STOLEN
FROM
PATRICIA
BRADBURY

·THE GEHENNA PRESS · THE WORK OF FIFTY YEARS·

·1942·1992·

THE CATALOGUE OF AN EXHIBITION
CURATED BY LISA UNGER BASKIN
CONTAINING AN ASSESSMENT
OF THE WORK OF THE PRESS
BY COLIN FRANKLIN
A BIBLIOGRAPHY OF THE BOOKS
OF THE GEHENNA PRESS
BY HOSEA BASKIN
& NOTES ON THE BOOKS
BY THE PRINTER
LEONARD BASKIN

THE BRIDWELL LIBRARY
&
THE GEHENNA PRESS

PARTICIPATING INSTITUTIONS

THE BRIDWELL LIBRARY
SOUTHERN METHODIST UNIVERSITY
DALLAS · TEXAS

THE GROLIER CLUB
NEW YORK · NEW YORK

THE UNIVERSITY OF DELAWARE LIBRARY
NEWARK · DELAWARE

CARNEGIE MELLON UNIVERSITY LIBRARIES
PITTSBURGH · PENNSYLVANIA

THE JOHN HAY LIBRARY
BROWN UNIVERSITY
PROVIDENCE · RHODE ISLAND

THE ROBERT W. WOODRUFF LIBRARY
EMORY UNIVERSITY
ATLANTA · GEORGIA

PRINCETON UNIVERSITY LIBRARY
THE LEONARD L. MILBERG GALLERY FOR THE GRAPHIC
ARTS · RARE BOOKS & SPECIAL COLLECTIONS
PRINCETON · NEW JERSEY

THE LIBRARY OF CONGRESS
WASHINGTON · D · C ·
A SPECIAL EXHIBITION

BEINECKE RARE BOOK & MANUSCRIPT LIBRARY
YALE UNIVERSITY
NEW HAVEN · CONNECTICUT

Distributed by the
University Press of New England
Hanover and London

Library of Congress
Catalog Card No. 91-77797
ISBN 0-941881-09-1
©1992 The Gehenna Press &
The Bridwell Library

FOREWORD

The Bridwell, divinity library of this university, has since its beginnings in 1950 been devoted to books well made. Its founder, Joseph Sterling Bridwell, and the first librarian, Decherd Turner, believed the library should be noted for those fine editions which record our best human hopes, faith, and traditions. Very early on such books made by Leonard Baskin came to the library in the Levi A. Olan Collection, a gift honoring the distinguished Dallas citizen and erudite rabbi of Temple Emanu-el.

We clearly feel that Mr. Baskin's work is integral to the first interests of this library. What he has designed, cut, pressed and pulled over fifty years is most often invitation–never dainty or pretty, but frontal and awe-striking–to break beyond comfortable and familiar dimensions to a world where myths, both dark and bright, enfold unsuspected "layers of meaning." Baskin's art does not engage the trivial; he, whether it be in prints, type, or sculpture, is monumental. And, through that grandeur and formality he lends us intimations of that which he has termed "hidden puissance" and "veiled vitality."

Thus, The Elizabeth Prothro Galleries of The Bridwell Library welcome this generous reflection on what Leonard Baskin has achieved in the fifty years of the Gehenna Press. Indeed, the library is privileged to be able to assist in this catalogue and the exhibition which travels from here across the United States.

Robert Maloy
The J.S. Bridwell Foundation Librarian
Southern Methodist University
Dallas, Texas

ACKNOWLEDGEMENTS

Assembling this exhibition was various and complex, revelatory, and, at times, difficult. Kenneth Shure was crucial to its success. His tenacious and persistent commitment to The Gehenna Press as both collector, and representative over the past six years has in no small measure insured that what began as an idea that he and I discussed one evening in the library at Leeds would culminate in this celebratory fiftieth anniversary exhibition. The concern, steadfastness and skill with which he negoiated the myriad mechanics of the exhibition, from dealing with participating institutions, shippers, contracts, lawyers, insurers, printers et al cannot be acknowledged any more deeply than I do now.

I wish to thank Dr. Robert Maloy, the J.S. Bridwell Foundation Librarian, Southern Methodist University, Roberta Cox, Coordinator of Public Programs, and Jon Speck, Exhibition Designer, for their continuous and generous support of both the exhibition and this catalogue. Colin Franklin, scholar and student of the private press has written an illuminating and keen assessment of the work of The Gehenna Press. It was a delight to have Charlotte and Colin Franklin in residence at Leeds as he worked in the early wintry morning hours surrounded by stacks of Gehenna Press books and ephemera on the library table.

Hosea Baskin assumed the enormous task of writing the definitive bibliography of The Gehenna Press, from 1942 through 1992. It fell to him to make order from the not so orderly production of the press, to count and collate, puzzle and identify typefaces, papers, pressmarks, varients and other vagaries of a press, until recently, concerned with production rather than with punctilious record keeping.

I am very grateful to Stephen Brook and Jeffrey Dwyer who produced the original bibliography of The Gehenna Press in 1975. Gray Parrot, binder to the press, patiently answered questions at all hours; David P. Becker, print curator & connoiseur and Wyman Parker, Librarian Emeritus, Olin Library, Wesleyan University, generously lent bibliographic notes of their own extensive work on Gehenna; Philip Isaacson, counsel to the press has graciously provided assistance when called upon.

Sidney Kaplan, editor of The Gehenna Press, has willingly and generously contributed his time and energy in myriad ways, I am grateful to him and to Emma Nogrady Kaplan. Richard Michelson, Michael Kuch and Arthur Larson have all contributed to the success of the exhibit in various ways as have David Bourbeau, Rebecca Fay, Eric Vellert and Anne Harrison, my thanks to them and to Noel Chanan, of London, England, for his photograph of Leonard Baskin taken in the winter of 1991 in the pressroom at Leeds. Thanks to David Block for his enthusiastic support, and to Mimi and Arnold Elkind and Priscilla Juvelis for their commitment to the press.

I am enormously grateful to the various institutions and private collectors who have given reality to the exhibition by graciously consenting to loans from their collections. I wish to thank Alice D. Schreyer, former Assistant of Libraries for Special Collections, Susan Brynteson, Director of Libraries, and Timothy Murray, Head of Special Collections, University of Delaware; Dr. Linda Matthews, Librarian, Robert W. Woodruff Library, Emory University; Thomas J. Michalak, former Director, University Libraries, and Mary Catharine Johnsen, Special Collections Librarian, Carnegie Mellon University; Martin Hutner, and Kimball Higgs, The Grolier Club; Jennifer B. Lee, Curator of Printed Books, John Hay Library, Brown University; Dale Roylance, Curator of Graphic Arts, Princeton University Library; Ruth Mortimer, acting Librarian and Curator of Rare Books and Special Collections, and Karen Kukil, Assistant of Curator Rare Books, Neilson Library, Smith College; Larry Sullivan, Chief of Rare Books and Special Collections Division, and Peter VanWingen, Specialist for the Book Arts, The Library of Congress.

The special exhibition at the Library of Congress is drawn from its own extensive holdings of The Gehenna Press augmented by preparatory material from private collections.

Particular thanks to Vincent Giroud, Curator of Modern Books and Manuscripts, and the staff at the Beinecke Rare Book and Manuscript Library, Yale University, for providing pleasant and easy access that helped facilitate my work sorting through the boxed papers of The Gehenna Press which are part of the Baskin Deposit, at the Beinecke Library. Donald R. McClelland, of the Smithsonian Traveling Exhibition Service provided useful information; and thanks to Tom Johnson and Anita Walker Scott at the University Press of New England, the distributors of this catalogue. Linda Figovsky did an exemplary job of typesetting both for the catalogue and the exhibition.

Roberta Bannister and Gail Alt of the Oxbow Press, for their commitment to excellence and their constant pursuit of perfection in producing this catalogue; for their patience, skill, keen eyes, and especially for their and Blanche's friendship, I thank them profoundly.

And lastly to Leonard for his prodigious and glorious Gehenna Press, which he often reminds me is really "only a peripheral, though splendid, activity", my thanks and my love.

Lisa Unger Baskin
Curator of the Exhibition.

LENDERS TO THE EXHIBITION

JOHN HAY LIBRARY · BROWN UNIVERSITY
CARNEGIE MELLON UNIVERSITY LIBRARIES
THE LIBRARY OF CONGRESS
UNIVERSITY OF DELAWARE LIBRARY
NEILSON LIBRARY · SMITH COLLEGE
BRIDWELL LIBRARY · SOUTHERN METHODIST UNIVERSITY
BEINECKE RARE BOOK & MANUSCRIPT LIBRARY · YALE UNIVERSITY
LUCRETIA BASKIN
HOSEA BASKIN & SARAH BUTTENWIESER
TOBIAS BASKIN & LAURA GREEN
LISA UNGER BASKIN
DAVID P. BECKER
RONALD COHEN
NEIL ELLIOTT
DEBORAH AND PHILIP ISAACSON
MATA AND ARTHUR JAFFEE
EMMA AND SIDNEY KAPLAN
MICHAEL KUCH
JANET AND JOHN MARQUSEE
GRAY PARROT AND CHRISTINE JON COVERT
PEARL AND NORMAN RABINOWITZ
KENNETH AND PETER SCHRAGER
LIV ROCKEFELLER AND KENNETH SHURE
ESTELLE G. UNGER

Photo by Noel Chanan

FIFTY YEARS OF THE GEHENNA PRESS
BY COLIN FRANKLIN

In Leonard Baskin's seventieth year, viewing this exhibition which represents the first half century of his Gehenna Press, it is interesting to reflect that a century ago (1891) the first Kelmscott book appeared from the press of William Morris. Though a temptation towards large comparisons should be avoided one may view the Gehenna achievement in that context, against the background of typographic reform, bibliophile taste, artistic work, bearing in mind always that for Baskin these books display just one facet of an artist's life. Nobody can tell whether he will be remembered a century hence as sculptor, print-maker, draughtsman, illustrator, author, or creator of the Gehenna Press.

Kelmscott books appeared during the last five years of Morris's life, and two after his death; the Ashendene Press, most constant and varied of them all, ran for about four decades from 1895; if we take 1942 as the starting date for Gehenna it has outlived them all. If time is no measure of excellence, a first look at the books exhibited shows their total range from small to vast, from typographic ballet to conventional text, expressionist monotypes to such delicate etching as compares with the work of Dutch masters from the seventeenth century. In this half century Baskin has explored the ground, planted his garden; at seventy he knows it, but leaves us guessing which part he will choose to cultivate next. Behind his enormous achievement lies the endearing diffidence and uncertainty which caused him to describe himself as 'an artist who feels isolated and under seige'. Books might provide an exit from privacy, yet 'People like me', he said in a recent interview, 'who care about printing, constitute the tiniest lunatic fringe in the nation'.

The large estate of Gehenna books, and varied terrain where they have thrived, make this a difficult essay to write. The focus of a private press tends to be upon typography or illustration or text, but Gehenna has explored them all and excelled in each. The ground should be described a little, for this to be understood.

I have known Leonard Baskin for twenty-five of his fifty printing years, as artist and incomparable collector. I am not competent to write about his art, beyond declaring that if I were able to own the works of one living artist I would choose his. Seeing sympathetic bronzes of burdened old men spaced about the lawn of his English garden, it was easy to feel a collector's desire such as is not inspired by the angled girders and rusting abstractions familiar in many a university campus or upon forecourts of a thousand public buildings. One could also appreciate the solitude involved in so distancing himself from modern movements. Here was originality within a tradition, moving and comprehensible as the work of Rodin.

As to his drawings, I had first come upon them in 1962 when the University of Chicago invited him to illustrate a new translation of the Iliad; in that book they were much reduced. I viewed the drawings by chance at the Sterling Library in Yale where they were exhibited. They possessed the astonishing force and suffering I now associate with his work and that of Kathe Kollwitz.

Baskin's chronic addiction as collector of books and prints is very relevant to any account of books he has printed, for they also grew within traditions. It is a commonplace of collecting, rare of attainment now, that no form of life in libraries compares with the intimacy of owning. The point has to be made, because the books and prints surrounding him are also within the soul of that art which informs this exhibition.

It was and remains possible for him to collect thus, though seeking always his own discoveries; where these coincided with common taste the regrettable overlap was often somehow conquered. I first saw his library through an unforgettable winter night in Massachusetts. Apart from the surprises he had managed a powerful presence of Blake.

Gerard Manley Hopkins praised 'all things counter, original, spare, strange'; the phrase recalls my impression of the many treasures brought out to view that night, which being so identified with his life have also become part of his work. Three veins of discovery remain especially vivid, in the bizarre anatomic mezzotints of the Gautier D'Agoty family, colour-printed in the eighteenth century, and two other glorious assemblies of colour printing: a mass of chiaroscuro woodcuts from that period back to the early sixteenth century, and a very complete collection, in many states of trial and proof, of the work of Ploos van Amstel.

Powerful collections in different veins surrounded him then and since, have come and gone, but colour-printing and the grotesque form a prevailing presence through his art and in the Gehenna Press; indeed it becomes foolish to suggest any clear distinction between his books and art. When is a book not a book?

> Bless them all, bless them all,
> The long and the short and the tall.

ran the chorus of a wretched wartime song, apt for Gehenna books which have upon occasion been long, emerge from a tall phase now, but rejoiced at first in a particular form of smallness which has never departed; for Baskin, to quote a finer poem then the war-time lyric, has been able

> To see a World in a Grain of Sand
> And a Heaven in a Wild Flower.
> Hold Infinity in the palm of your hand
> And Eternity in an hour.

With such perception of smallness it is not surprising that in his library was a substantial collection of early emblem books, of etchings by Callot and Della Bella, work from such 'Little Masters' as Hans Sebald Beham, and etchings of extreme delicacy from the Dutch seventeenth century. In this dimension he has constantly observed and worked, whatever the overall size of Gehenna books in which the results appear.

All things counter, original, spare, strange. They were to be found in his collection of books on perspective; in the grotesques of wood and metal ornament present in his assembly of old pattern books; in whatever obscure place an artist took the chance to create unexpected fantasy.

Visitors who see in this exhibition a puzzling variety of form and mood would discover the same qualities in Baskin's conversation and his writing, which also change from simplicity to idiosyncratic convolution. It is a consistent aspect of his taste for the baroque. Take for instance a sentence about Peter Flotner, portrayed in the *Icones Librorum Artifices*: 'In poses of contraposto sinuosity, of serpentine deformity, Flotner's plaques of Sibyls & prophets, of eremites & martyrs, gods & apostles, betray their mannerist origins'. In the design of a book, as of a sentence, he has often chosen shape before sense; words are split absurdly, for geometric effect. All this, as he knew and enjoys, opposes whatever was taught in the first week of every course in graphic design or written English. Perversity is a privilege of the private press. He also knows directness. 'I don't think *Icones* could have been done' he said, waving to shelves of his elegant earlier books, 'unless I'd done all the crap that's in here'. Both traits exist in his own vital emblem of the Crow: 'I like them because they are disliked'.

Names, titles, emblems. A line from the first Book of *Paradise Lost* gave the Press its title:
>And black Gehenna call'd, the type of Hell.
By some strange coincidence, in Northampton Baskin met Sidney Kaplan, a professor of English at the University of Massachusetts, fascinated like him by type, who in his salad days had set up poems and broadsides under a similar name, the Hellgate Press. Kaplan would play an important part in the early Gehenna years.

The Press was called Eremite for a couple of years after Baskin's return to the United States. The old form of 'Hermit' suggesting privacy was also typical of his avoidance of the obvious. His most frequently used symbol has been the pomegranate, which Persephone carried to hell—and, fertile with seed ready to fall, it happens also to be a Jewish symbol. So with Crow whom nobody loves, Persephone's pomegranate, the hidden Eremite and Hell itself, it takes no special insight to perceive an undertow of pessimism. One could say, too, that a good printer aims to achieve black.

And the first paradox of Baskin's printing is that no artist in type ever showed such delight in colour, printer's flowers and borders, titles, five colours patterned on a page with such constant control that the thought of excess never till this moment of denial entered my head. There it stands to puzzle us, one man expressing a spectrum of responses, heavy dark woodcuts of Crow, and the Garden-of-Eden summer of two books with characteristically remote titles, as if half-ashamed to confess their innocence, *Cancelleresca Bastarda Displayed in a Series of Maxims and Mottos* (1965), and *Flosculi Sententiarum* (1967).

As the exhibition celebrates fifty years it is appropriate to look at the first book, printed when Baskin was a student at the Yale School of Art, bearing in mind that the next would not appear for another nine years; and to note the presence of those constant qualities which characterise that first phase of the press and continue to inform the folios which come from it now, smallness and colour. Well leaded, set in eight point Caslon to the right of a page which could have held two or three columns, the poems are alternately red and black; the title, small in a vast space, also has two colours. Printed on hand-made papers which differ in size and texture, the margins also vary by nearly two inches. This sophisticated mannerism declares a bibliophile experience of handling old books in shops or the Sterling Library at Yale. One notes without surprise a similar contrast of mood in the poems, from one which begins:

'eyes in misery swell to burst with fury
from their sockets, and roll into some
filth and gaze no more from pits
of hell upon agonies that are man . . .'
to another in happier spirit:
'Mountain top annointed
with mist's
Kiss. . . .
And my heart goes out and lies
breathing with the lit moon'.

In 1951 the press stirred to life again with *A Little Book of Natural History Engravings by Leonard Baskin,* unbound, playful, dismissed by him now but rich with the shape of things to come, linocuts printed red, green or black, his bestiary, with a black and melancholy Man of Peace on the title page. Neither then nor since has there been any fast distinction between his books and separate editions of prints.

The early Gehenna books were printed at different presses and in several places, as Baskin moved from a teaching job at Worcester Art Museum to become Professor of Art at Smith College, gained experience with Richard Warren at the Metcalf Printing and Publishing Company in Northampton and acquired his own equipment to print at home. Any quibble as to which texts and images were done on the hand press and which from a Vandercook proofing press or by offset lithography is of bibliographic interest not central to the Gehenna story. In an unpublished essay Baskin has made his statement: 'I find the prejudice for letter-press and against offset ludicrous and absurd. One must, I think, be concerned with those typographic verities of clarity, cogency, wit, grace, strength and comeliness and not be pre-occupied with process'.

Through two decades of the early Gehenna years, from 1956 to 1976, shortly after Leonard and Lisa Baskin moved to England,

Harold McGrath was engaged as pressman. The press has been fortunate in its pressmen: McGrath in Northampton, Robert Wakefield after the move to England and latterly Arthur Larson in Hadley. It would be more true to say that those who worked there learned to do what Baskin wanted, as Binning, Hooper, Gage-Cole, comparable technicians in England a century ago, learnt to do what Morris and Walker asked. McGrath, never a designer, achieved the shaped pages and perfect register demanded for many title pages and such works of art as *Flosculi Sententiarum*. In the Connecticut valley between Northampton and Mount Holyoke is an impressive accumulation of young printers, binders, process engravers, producing in peaceful surroundings work of the highest quality. Most of them learned from him, and now they contribute to his work. The artistic neighbourhood has a faintly feudal air.

But the presence of a pressman caused problems in keeping the press busy; Baskin recalls that for stretches of time it was idle, and this in part explains the diversity of books through those years. Some reflected his interest as artist or collector: assemblies of prints, in portfolio or bound, with or without title pages; groups of portraits, real or imagined; fantasies, caprices, demons; birds, beasts, dogs, insects; coins, culs de lampe. Several were typographic jeux d'esprit, more and less serious. A significant group came from the sympathetic advice of Sidney Kaplan whose position as literary editor gave scope to the social views they shared and assuaged a hint of guilt, Baskin confesses, in the self-indulgent notion of any private printing.

The Kaplan effect, commendable, scholarly, visually excellent, is less likely now to tempt venial collectors than are other veins of Gehenna printing; the prime movers look back with some pride to achievements which will serve them at the Day of Judgement—save them from Gehenna perhaps—but wanderers among book-shops and auctions (through this exhibition also perhaps) make their way surely as horned beetles or diptera towards coloured shapes of type and the small brilliant etchings.

Blake and the Youthful Ancients, 1956, was the last book printed by Baskin himself before the advent of McGrath, and first among a succession of largely imagined portraits. These small woodcut ideas of a circle he greatly reveres, its triangular typeset title, minimal explanation, set tones and themes which would develop across the future. Two years later *Horned Beetles and Other Insects,* only thirty copies, a series of etchings 'printed from the plates by the artist with the assistance of Louis Smith', was a wonderful leap into the best Gehenna vein which continues to delight those few who manage to discover it. He had found a tray of specimens (still extant) and a modern book on the species, but the etchings extend to those qualities of detail, colour, texture, life-in-death, which his best work offered from that day to this. 'On a variety of European and Japanese handmade papers', says the colophon: these papers assist, with wide but not extravagant margins; yet only an intimacy with texture in some eighteenth-century colour printing, and with the Dutch seventeenth-century etchers, and his own genius could produce *Horned Beetles.* McGrath printed the small red interleaving titles. When is a book not a book? This has title page, a sentence from Darwin, colophon, no elevation or tedium of reading.

There were other groups of beasts, *Caprices* on varied papers, the slum dogs of Castle Street in Worcester, Mass. preoccupied with their obscenities and protected by huge margins, and two charming small books which cast their light towards future events: *Culs de Lampe,* 1968, reproduced photographically with many colours and papers from headpieces and decorations in old books which had pleased him; and a typical minor piece sent out at Easter 1965, coins and medals printed deeply–embossed–in a variety of colours or upon coloured papers, with a paragraph from Addison's 'Dialogues upon the Usefulness of Ancient Medals'. This simple greeting was given a latin title, *Nummus Consulum Romanorum.*

Several more serious productions from that time suggest the later scale of Gehenna books. *Laus Pictorum: Portraits of Nineteenth Cen-*

tury Artists Invented and Engraved by Leonard Baskin, 1969, is a remarkable book, unbound in chemise and box, in an edition of three hundred and fifty copies split into three groups according to French rather than American or English custom–a gesture towards the *livre de peintre* with its *justification de tirage*. The large quarto has a disparate assembly of fifteen artist portraits, etched and woodcut mostly black on different papers, matted and mounted to be seen through windows of the album leaves. This powerful work, with prefatory paragraphs about each artist, looks forward to the *Icones*. A private printer gathers the artists who happen to be present within his brain.

Terminalia, 1972, small folio in a small edition of thirty-five copies, has eight etchings of fictitious stone figures of 'the god who marks the boundaries of the tilled land'; with a passage from Ovid which explains their meaning, in Latin and Sir James Frazer's translation. This is very Baskin, informed by the bookish past, a minor vehicle for his imagination. The theme continues.

A third and very large achievement, which he tends to regard as his typographic masterpiece, is the *Hippolytos* of Euripides in Robert Bagg's translation, an edition of two hundred copies, 1969. Here are tall pages of purest classic setting, the Centaur type of Bruce Rogers, followed by Baskin's etchings in a separate portfolio. It was and remains a fine work, his homage to Bruce Rogers; yet if one looks ahead this leads towards a less happy venture, the two Gehenna Shakespeare volumes. The habit of enormous pages had found scope six years earlier in *Encantadas: Two Sketches from Herman Melville's Enchanted Isles with Woodcuts by Rico Lebrun.* Shaped, red-starred, dense, dazzling, this also must be reckoned a visual book with French-style *justification de tirage*–five with a second suite on Japanese paper, an original drawing, and so forth. General acclaim and the technical display may bring a sense that huge is brilliant, but *Encantadas* makes one look back with new respect to *Horned Beetles* and the little Blake woodcuts.

A style of inconspicuous binding, appropriate to the varied format and forceful illustration of Gehenna books, was evident from early years in the work of Arno Werner. It continues to this day, generally but not always through his pupil Gray Parrot. Baskin has cogent views upon binding: 'an upstart incursion into the whole meaning of the books'; they should relate to content 'in a very decorous way'. Gehenna books were commonly issued bound or in boxes, and there have been few special bindings. It has always been a problem, between reason and taste and expense. French artist-books came boxed, for bindings to be commissioned; two and three centuries ago shops sold books in paper or boards, for binding to order, and the few volumes which survive thus now are treasured. Most of the printing-revival presses chose simple paper board or limp vellum, and among those which flew higher perhaps only Nonesuch and Gregynog were successful. Gehenna bindings from Arno Werner and Gray Parrot, under Baskin's critical eye, are a rare delight in form, material, lettering, and acceptance of his caveat that each should relate to content in a very decorous way. Small lettering at the head and tail, square joints and the discreet use of marbled papers leave no cause for cavil or complaint.

It would be false to suppose any absolute exists dividing visual from literary Gehenna books. In producing texts of social or artistic relevance as part of the policy of publishing and keeping the pressman busy, editor and owner accepted a temptation which afflicts publishers: no less than four series were started, none of which progressed far. *Gehenna Essays in Art* managed three charming books with excellent illustrations, in numbers which declined from an optimistic five hundred *(Francesco Laurana)* to one hundred and fifty *(The Drawings of Jacob de Gheyn)*. *Gehenna Tracts* also stopped after three, the *Gehenna Shakespeare* ran to two volumes and *Gehenna Poets* one. All were worth doing, sale is no measure of merit, but duty takes a less beguiling form than love. Standards never dropped. A sense of strain, of striving for effect through size, shows through the two large Shakespeare plays, *Titus Andronicus* and *Othello,* both chosen no doubt for the obscurely social reason that their heroes or villains happen to be black. Neither stimulated much interest in artist or outside world, and size started to assume a hint of bombast.

Tracts and *Essays in Art* deserved to go further, but the real world of publishing called a halt. Many plates of drawings by Jacob de Gheyn were printed by Meriden under Harold Hugo immaculately; John Woolman's two Tracts on the Keeping of Negroes, in Centaur on Fabriano paper, have three-colour title pages within borders of characteristic Baskin charm. Two hundred and thirty bi-lingual pages of Goethe's *West-Ostlicher Divan* kept pressman rather than bookshops busy, which of course casts no criticism upon that volume with drawings by Baskin, three hundred copies, 1970. *The Defense of Gracchus Babeuf,* 1964, was a step in commendable political and aesthetic directions, issued as folded folio sheets in morocco chemise, cloth folder and box by Arno Werner, with Thomas Cornell's etched portraits loose on blue paper in their places. Edmund Wilson in *To the Finland Station* had mentioned Babeuf's noble plea for liberty during his trial, 1797, but it had never been translated into English. 'After the Apology of Socrates before the Jury of Five Hundred', said the prospectus, 'Babeuf's plea before the tribunal of the Directory during the final hours of the French Revolution is perhaps the most splendid testament ever uttered in behalf of the freedom of man's mind'. Three hundred copies were printed, prices ranging from three hundred dollars to six hundred and fifty; eleven years later it had not sold out, but the least edition was raised to five hundred dollars and the middle by optimism in despair multiplied threefold to fifteen hundred.

This essay is not concerned with the economics of the Press, except to notice high ideals in an unfriendly commercial world. A private press may do, Gehenna has done, what it likes; every good reason supports a fine academic production on hand-made paper, yet one seeks a certain idiosyncrasy in these realms and with relief discovers it in another kind of Gehenna book which expresses more matter and less art.

Both were present, the purpose literary, in an amusing early production hand-printed in 1953, John Skelton's bawdy ballad *The Tunning of Elynour Rummynge*. The Press has thus two poets laureate in its history. Baskin's coloured wood engravings which include a Castle Street dog eloquently echoed the poem. At the other border of refinement is Blake's *Auguries of Innocence,* done for the Print Club of Philadelphia in 1959. Baskin's emblematic iconography, a second colour, Italian hand-made paper and the poem itself raise this high among Gehenna minor pieces. A comparable instance, Poe's short essay called *Anastatic Printing,* conveys the fun editor and artist had, one discovering the forgotten work, the other designing and illustrating it. The semi-nonsense of Poe's essay appealed to Baskin whose colour-printed portrait of the author was 'achieved anastatically' as the colophon, after correcting a spelling mistake, reveals. The word meant relief-etching; his trial in this difficult technique is mounted on the title page. Among serious contributions from the early days was a large quarto *Thirteen Poems by Wilfred Owen* whose work had at that time *(1956)* received no American edition. 'I've learnt a lot about printing since then', Baskin says, but heavy Caslon type balances Ben Shahn's drawings which were printed by Meriden. Copyright trouble came from Owen's executors, but 'I was in a passion, I didn't want permission'.

Two other contrasting volumes end this wander across early Gehenna work dismissed by its master in a vivid phrase quoted earlier. *A Check List of the Publications of Thomas Bird Mosher,* 1966, printed on beautiful Fabriano paper (wind-dried, unpressed) shows masterly treatment of many awkward problems through the length of a substantial work. It is perhaps the most satisfying among textual Gehenna books, simple in perfect taste. Very different with three text and three preliminary leaves is the little *Scholastic*

Dialogue translated from Alcuin, opening in blue and red:

PIPPIN   What is a letter?
ALCUIN   The guardian of history.
PIPPIN   What is a word?
ALCUIN   The expositor of the mind.

Twenty-five copies were printed in 1968. It could be an emblem for the Press, perfection in a small compass. The title page has only the initial GP, blue above printer's flowers of red and green.

At this time of writing, as snow covers hills and hollows, the Gehenna Press finds itself in a phase of large books; not quite so tall as *Encantadas* or *Hippolytos,* but generally in another area from the work of Callot, Della Bella, Jean De Tournes which had earlier informed it. The collecting influence is at work again, for Baskin has taken to old portrait books which often filled great folios. He owns the magnificant *Fuggerorum et Fuggerarum . . . . . Imagines* for instance, 1618, members of the wealthy banking family surrounded by wonderfully elaborate baroque cartouches; the little-known Heince and Bignon folio from 1655, of 'Hommes Illustres François' within little etchings of events and scenes from their lives; and most apt *Le Mareschal de Bataille,* 1647, in which engravings of soldiers at drill are followed by battle-order diagrams in two-colour formations of geometric dots, 'pure op-art' as he points out, and three-colour schematic arrangements of guns.

Delicacy in large folio characterises the latter-day Gehenna books, recalling Baskin's phrases in the *Icones* about Etienne Delaune, that he was 'a brilliant and inventive ornamentalist and entirely convincing in the tiniest of formats'; for the paradox is that he has taken to producing miniature work in rather large format, and again one looks to the collecting spirit for some rational understanding.

Though rarity has no artistic merit, it is a rare bibliophile who remains indifferent to large margins, uncut edges, coloured inks and unexpected papers; so the creator of these recent books, who suffers incurably from bibliomania, lets rip with a freedom few contrive to indulge. 'I always tried,' he says, 'to use the best hand-made paper if I could afford it'; so far so good, but beyond that stance he concludes now 'the Press could only exist commercially in the most outré snobbish way'. And before expanding or expounding I can declare total support for the most outré snobbish way.

It was an interesting if unguarded comment, from knowledge that books made in his freedom of private taste in small numbers sell expensively to the few; the Press enjoys for the first time in its history a period of success, recognition, acclaim. If this in its turn were to bring any hint of an assumption that slender work in large format and small numbers is itself a formula for success this whole endeavour would be set on a dangerous course, for collectors are sensitive to cynicism. My guess, right or wrong before the fiftieth anniversary, is that the books will again become small as *Horned Beetles* or *Blake and the Youthful Ancients*.

Meanwhile we view with gratitude a spate of marvellous Gehenna work which has flooded the decade since one tall octavo *A Primer of Birds,* 1981, in which Baskin's woodcuts illustrated poems by Ted Hughes–'the great period of the Press', as he regards it. That was the start, two hundred and fifty copies 'printed at the Gehenna Press, Lurley in Devon'. For nine years after 1975 the Baskins lived at an enchanting small Jacobean manor house, grey stone and peace itself, a few miles west of Tiverton. It was possible for me to travel from Oxford for lunch and, in that regrettable period of less attention to the dangers of good claret before a journey, to drive and dream my way home in a haze of old books and new. Crossing the small stream, up a steep lane to Lurley, one entered a magic place which almost exists again, as if the ghost had gone west, in Massachusetts.

A Primer of Birds was a curious reopening after five years of silence, printed on an old Columbian press in the garden shed, black powerful woodcuts illustrating poems by Ted Hughes who lived half an hour further west. It was an old friendship. In 1958 Hughes had taught at the University of Massachusetts, his wife Sylvia Plath at Smith College in Northampton where Baskin lived; now they chose Devon, to be near him. A Ted Hughes poem, *Pike,* had been printed among the earliest Gehenna broadsides, 1959. From very different backgrounds their minds have worked in artistic harmony: Baskin's Crow drawings inspired the whole Crow mythology of Ted Hughes. *Cave Birds* had appeared in 1979 from Scolar Press, the large limited version followed by a trade edition, but with the Columbian established at Lurley there was no more need for outsiders. In small light type the poems travel unexpectedly far down the narrow page, each woodcut gives a black shock. The Gehenna Press in perspective has never been merely visual; *A Primer of Birds* was its diffident apt re-entry.

A Gehenna Alphabet, 1982, seems relatively minor but seventeen copies of an almost unknown work, called appropriately *Unknown Dutch Artists*—unissued, undistributed, every thinkable negative, experimental and wittily inventive, were printed in 1983. Forming a Gehenna collection would be cruel work, but any collector could reckon himself happiest in discovering this book[1] which made as sudden a leap within its period as had *Horned Beetles* a quarter of a century before. These thirteen 'Etchings and Biographical Notices', small and very small on a variety of papers, in several colours, reflect at once his reading and writing and collecting: little portraits of nobody, in the language of art history which becomes also his convoluted game of words shaped about or beneath each. Perhaps it does not matter whether these vigorous little people existed or not; they lived while he imagined them, ghosts from the collective past of print-making, report neither less nor more interesting than research, their darkness like that of Romeyn Houtlucht 'rarely lit by Fortuna's revolving searchlight and then made Lambent only by the Luminescent presence of Hercules Seghers'. That most people know no more of Seghers, pioneer of color printing, whose very rare work has elud-

---

[1] I have not collected Gehenna books, and do not own it.

ed even Baskin's vigilance, than of Houtlucht whose face and name were invented for the occasion, is a trivial footnote in the history of art. After twisting the page to read about Magdalena Ruysch, her forbidding face viewed through a cutout oval, who 'expended her entire artistry in limning her father's "Anatomisch Kabinet", replete with numerous bizarre and didactic composi-tions... bought by Peter the Great during his second visit to Amsterdam and removed to St. Petersburg in 1717', tragedy follows. 'Along with the exhibits went the wondrous drawings, that were the life-work of Magdelena Ruysch. The sailors on the dark and perilous voyage, drank the preserving fluids from out of the jars, and no trace has ever been discovered of either specimens or drawings'.

Total nonsense? No, the Kabinet existed and Peter bought it; that tale of the sailors may be legend. Baskin owns the *Werken van Fredrik Ruysch,* 1744, including *Alle d'Anatomische Cabinetten* with its engraved tableaux vivants, animated moralised arrangements of foetal skeletons, diseased stones, cancers, lungs, arteries, an ephemeron as emblem of life's brevity. Leopardi wrote a poem in which these dead limbs lived—Baskin dreamed up the fictitious series of drawings by a non–existent daughter. It becomes a game of true or false, descending to the dark postage-stamp-size etching of Joos de Boem on a larger area of orange flanked by the briefest description: 'No works by Joos de Boem have thus far been identified'.

It led to a work of real homage, indistinguishable from the false, *Icones Librorum Artifices,* 1988, thirty-two etched portraits most of which were colour-printed or on tinted grounds, from Jean de Tournes and Crispin van de Passe to Alan Odle and Marcus Behmer, an edition of forty copies upon large untrimmed papers. Familiar ingredients are here, in different array: shaped type, broken words, windows, colour, minature art upon massive margin. You take your pick, as he took his; I choose from among them Johannes Teyler, seventeenth-century artist of colour printing à la poupée, and an obscure fellow called Jan Kleurprent 'who constituted the arching connection between Leblon & D'Agoty', because my first meeting with Baskin also introduced them. His unusual scholarship dances in a ballet of improbable prose. *Icones,* as happens from time to time, was promptly hailed as his masterpiece.

In 1983 one more work had been printed in Devonshire, *Diptera, a Book of Flies and Other Insects,* reopening the vein which produced *Horned Beetles,* showing that the same blood flowed, an exceedingly delicate display of texture colour and technique. Forty-five copies were done, including ten on 'different papers & in variant colours'. The occasional *tirage de tête,* a pleasant feature of certain Gehenna books, called for inventiveness because ordinary editions commonly came on different papers and in variant colours.

The Baskins returned to Massachusetts in 1984, issuing in the next several years an amazing sequence of books. In 1985 came *Mokomaki,* its bizarre theme briefly explained in a subtitle 'thirteen etchings of shrunken & tattooed Maori heads' and three poems by Ted Hughes who had in fact written poems for each head but only three were used. This foray into a new aspect of death was inspired by an amateur Victorian anthropologist's book on the subject; the author, a senior army officer, had illustrated it, Baskin says, with 'photographs and bad drawings' which sparked his chronic fascination with the grotesque. *Mokomaki* was published in an edition of fifty copies printed on a variety of large papers, with ten extra suites and two more on vellum, a flawless venture into that awkward medium. This sparse but brilliant work would have benefitted from a historical introduction, and the interleaving of every poem; those three unexplained at the start are easily by-passed, but it was precious material which could have been read with the etchings.

Next year *Hermaika,* an extension from the earlier *Terminalia,* offered a series of imaginative drawings reproduced by photo-offset at the Oxbow Press at Amherst and one woodcut; seventy-five copies, a few with the woodcut hand-coloured. All very Baskin, it might have been offered with a few original drawings, sketches, something other than the lithographs and woodcut plain or coloured which were interesting enough but one begins a little greedily to expect more.

1988 was the *annus mirabilis* with six admirable Gehenna books including *Icones*. If a witless phrase or two were heard, like 'flooding the market', it deserved contempt; for we have seen a creative phase of Baskin's art producing a cascade of diverse technique and vision from experimental coloured monotypes to the intricate etching of *Irises*.

The large *Irises* quarto has no text; Baskin has made nothing more delicate than this. Pre-occupied in his sculpture with shapes of burden and death, the books seem sometimes to look like vacations, escapes; yet they come from the same man, informed by the past which he chose to collect, and 'by indirection find direction out'. If war and the holocaust haunt his other art, these show the reverse of the medal. He happens to like medals, and makes them. *Irises* opens now at an oval flower etched sepia upon ochre, emblem of that peace which the world cannot give. One need not accept his amiable insistence that the books and sculpture are of different worlds. This is not a botanical work; thirty-five copies were done, all of the etchings printed in two states, coloured according to Baskin rather than God. A yellow or blue morocco binding by Gray Parrot adds to the pleasure of this Eremite book.

Two collections of wild 'monotypes', necessarily in very small editions, completed that year's work. Partly a misnomer, for monotype by definition produces one print, by proofing lightly and then more heavily a series of impressions was achieved. *Twelve Sculptors, a Book of Monotypes with Short Notes on the Monotypes & the Sculptors* was issued in an edition of twenty-five copies. It came from the heart, though a reader may be vexed to find true faces called 'physiognomic actualities'. This different kind of portrait book is unpredictable as the medium, in which inks get squashed to surprising effect. Most of the prints, signed, numbered and titled by the artist, were also 'touched', a slightly disappointing necessity. *Recollected Fragments of Ornament & Grotesque. A Book of Monotypes* carried this technique into another of his favourite themes and completed the tally for 1988. Sometimes touched again, for better or worse, these emotional inventions recollected in tranquillity after visiting Florence were explained in a relatively straightforward introduction:

> 'The book is a remembered visual response to seven midsummer weeks spent in Florence. As one walks the Florentine streets, one's eye finds no easy rest as the city's architectural marvels crash into one's subdued retinas from every point of vantage. And everywhere the buildings are encrusted with ornament and grotesque. The architectural ornamental overlay is like an excess of jewels lavishly strewn upon an extravagant sixteenth century costume. The unbridled use of ornamentation encroaches upon one's consciousness and instills wonder at the delicious secularity that infused the architects and sculptors'.

Only fourteen copies were done, a curious evocation of gothic individuality, with a title page in etched definition.

Both themes, grotesque and ornament, came together next year in a book of etchings called *Fancies Bizarreries & Ornamented Grotesques,* a return of that precision which Baskin first showed in *Horned Beetles* and exercised in all his arrangements of type. This festival of controlled colour printing, of grotesque upon baroque geometry, expresses an originality within traditions which seems to create his best work. The impositions make new imagery. Thirty-five copies were done, including eight with extra suites and colourings. Goethe's essay on Arabesque was translated for the edition.

As the Gehenna Press has never allowed new literature to disappear below its horizon for long, in 1989 a large quarto volume of poems by James Baldwin was handsomely printed. At this moment of writing a major work of Baskin's woodcuts and Ted Hughes' poems, *Capriccio,* nears completion. Coloured woodcuts of the *Sibyls* will make another volume, and somewhere between here and eternity is a book of cats.

No brief record can embrace the extent and excellence of so much work across half a century. I have not done justice to the typography, a dreary theme for description but easy to exhibit. An intriguing aspect of that lies in one characteristic Baskin perversity, his taste for unjustified setting—no words broken by distracting hyphens—alternating with geometric shapes which torture to distraction any syllable striking the borderline.

Gehenna's achievement recalls the architecture of some ancient university, some of its buildings appealing to immediate taste, others appearing alien, but all fine examples of their kind. A private press whose long history includes exquisite small etching, wild monotypes and expressionist woodcut, delicate experiments with fleurons and shaped typography, colour-printing, art history, social conscience and an impressive list of new poetry, all in a context of scholarly recollection, must one day be seen to rest near to the summit of them all.

BIBLIOGRAPHY BY HOSEA BASKIN
NOTES ON THE BOOKS BY LEONARD BASKIN

Bibliographical information is given in the following format:
Number. Brook bibliography number, if different. Title.
Line by line transcription of the title page.
Description of any features of the book not clear from the title page.
Size [height x width] in inches. Number of leaves or sheets. If the book is printed in italic, on rectos only, in color, or if there are tissue guards bound in to protect prints, it is noted here.
Collation. The contents of the book are listed page by page. For books issued in sheets, the numbering refers to sheets, not pages. A few books are foliated, not paginated; this is noted within their entries. Blank leaves are indicated, but blank versos are omitted. Thus, the notation "(1) half title; (3) title page;" means that the verso (2) is blank. In unpaginated books the pages are numbered from the recto of the first leaf on which type appears. Unpaginated pages are indicated by parentheses around the page numbers. Thus, the notation "(7)-(16)" means that pages 7 & 16 are not numbered, but some or all of the pages in between are numbered, while the notation "(7-16)" means that all pages from 7 to 16 are not numbered. The use of pressmarks is noted; all pressmarks are reproduced at the end of the catalogue.
Transcription of the colophon. If the colophon is signed or numbered, it is noted here.
Typeface & paper, if not given in the colophon.
Information about illustrations, if it is not given in sufficient detail in the collation.
Limitation, if not given in the colophon.
Binding description.
Prospectus information.
Description of variants, where known. Unique variants are generally not described.
Any other pertinent information.
Description of trade editions.

1 · ON A PYRE OF WITHERED ROSES

ON A PYRE OF WITHERED ROSES ‖ *poems by* ‖ LEONARD
BASKIN ‖ *the gehenna press* ‖ *mcmxlii* [first & last lines in red]
9¼ x 11¼, oblong. 20 sheets, untrimmed. Printed on rectos only in
red & black.
CONTENTS: (1) title page; (2) epigraph; (3–20) text.
TYPE: Caslon; PAPER: Old Hampshire Bank.
40 copies printed.
Issued in sheets.
Printed at the Jonathan Edwards Press, Yale University. Very few
copies have survived. Some copies are 7¾ x 8¼, oblong.

*It would, I think, be useful to tell the tale of my happy defile into printing. The Yale Art School, where I
was a student just before & during the first years of WWII, was Beaux-Arts academic & retardiere: its
masters kept a dead tradition alive and ruthlessly so, they were brutal in asserting their notions, opinions
& attitudes. I was petulantly & zealously young & aggressively ardent. My crude makings bore little
resemblance to my lofty aspirations & conceptions. I was in a state of anticipatory arrogance. I had built a
drawing style compacted out of Rossettian pre-Raphaelitism & Botticellian neo-platonism. These ill-
drawn effusions were achieved in life-drawing class, deploying the lightest tonalities of pencilled
graphite. Along would come the hateful master & he would slash at my timid, pallid drawings with
heavy charcoal, correcting my mistakes & instructing me in the uselessness of cast shadows & other illu-
sionist & naturalist devices: I rebelled against the repulsive criticisms, I cherished my incompetence, I
nursed my bashed ego & I appeared at life-class less & less. There is at Yale a separate library housed
within Sterling; it is called the Linonian and Brothers Library & was founded in 1832. It is a benefaction, for its long nave-like room with chaplets is stuffed with soft, billowing, deep-seated armchairs &
sofas, & furnished with reading books of every possible devourable sort. I began burrowing through that
room & the essence of my education derives from two years in sharp attendance at that wonderful library.
One fair day, I chanced upon the shelves laden with books by & about William Blake. Confronting
Blake plain & unexpected was like being struck by a locomotive. Here was model, praxis, paradigm &
example, an artist & poet coupled. He made his own strange & marvellous books, their impact was over-
whelming & I determined to learn to print. Of the responses to the art school induced wretchedness, I
note an alarming amount of drinking & a more alarming writing of heaps of poetry. My guardian angel
somehow prevented me from imitating Blake's mysterious relief-etching technique, for it is certain that I
would have failed in the attempt to combine image & text in a single copper plate. Three of Yale's col-
leges had printing presses & I managed a relationship with the senior printer at Jonathan Edwards College who handed me a key and access to bliss. Into that garden-shed printing office I plunged & saw for
the first time a Chandler & Price foot-treadle press & handled Caslon types, decent English paper, &
they in consort with rich black ink & typewashes make the wonderful stink of a printing office. The burning desire to print, implanted by Blake, had so seized me, that no difficulty could stay my composing-*

sticked hand. My entire ignorance of printing history & my woeful innocence of all printing practice & procedure did not prevent me from leaping into that messy, soul-satisfying cauldron. I did somehow manage to set and print a book of my poetry; the true Gehenna Press incunabulum. The poems were drenched in post-adolescent angst, a bitter-sweet schlagzahne of miserable loneliness, arrogance, self-pity & abraded sensibilities. The filling of the empty vessel with a ballast of typographic history & historical imperatives & knowledge of craft took a considerable time, indeed, still goes forward. Quite soon after these first halting steps, I found myself in the U.S. Navy, where other concerns forced themselves upon my startled notice. But the fantasy of The Gehenna Press persisted, if somewhat vague & amorphous.

1951

2 · A LITTLE BOOK OF NATURAL HISTORY

A LITTLE BOOK ‖ OF NATURAL HISTORY ‖ ENGRAV-INGS [2 fleurettes] BY ‖ LEONARD BASKIN ‖ [engraving] ‖ THE GEHENNA PRESS ‖ WORCESTER ‖ 1951 [all type in red]
With 26 linoleum engravings, including those on the title page & cover label, 2 wood engravings *[Ravens & Beetle]* & a woodcut *[Armadillo.]*
9 x 7. 30 sheets. Printed on rectos only in various colors.
CONTENTS: (1) title page; (2) index; 3-29 engravings; (30) colophon, with pressmark I in red.
COLOPHON: *"of this edition of A Little Book of Natural History, 50 copies were printed of which this is No.   "* Colophon signed & numbered by LB.
TYPE: Forum; PAPER: Troya.
Laid into a portfolio of blue paper over boards, with paper labels on the front cover & spine.
15 artist's copies were also printed.

After the war, my energies were devoted to the larger task of becoming an artist & printing remained dormant through five years of study. It was upon returning from Europe to Worcester, Mass., that the old desire to print manifested itself. Alas, Worcester was bereft of the like of Jonathan Edwards printing offices & the second Gehenna book was printed at a commercial printer. It is odd that the press' first book was entirely free of images & that its second had no words. Was it prophetic of an insight I later had in re Blake, that when his poetry is at its greatest, the art is at its weakest [witness "The Tyger",] & the opposite [see "Jerusalem".] This incursion into Worcester's printing world resulted in the press acquiring its first printing impedimenta; all discards, an ancient half-arced or D-shaped Vandercook proofing press & a medley of poor & battered types.

1952

3 · SOME ENGRAVINGS BY LEONARD BASKIN

[6-inch row of fleurons] ‖ Some Engravings By Leonard Baskin ‖
[pressmark I] ‖ The Gehenna Press ‖ 1952 ‖ [6-inch row of fleurons]
[all in red]

With 17 wood engravings, each signed & titled by LB.

8 x 7¼. 20 leaves, untrimmed. Printed on rectos only in red &
black.

CONTENTS: (1) title page; (3-35) engravings; (37) colphon; 1 blank
leaf.

COLOPHON: "ten copies of this book have been printed from
the blocks by the artist using the vandercook proof press at the
gehenna press june 1952"

PAPER: Quasi-Japanese paper.

Sewn into grey boards, with wrappers of blue-grey paper, with LB
ENGRAVINGS in a box of fleurons printed on the front cover.

4 · CASTLE STREET DOGS

castle ‖ street ‖ dogs ‖ Wood Engravings by Leonard Baskin [lines
1-3 in purple]

7¾ x 7¼. 24 leaves, untrimmed. Printed on rectos only.

CONTENTS: 1 blank leaf; (1) title page; 1 blank leaf; (5) quotation
from Freud; 1 blank leaf; (9-35) engravings; 1 blank leaf; (39) colophon, with pressmark II in red; 3 blank leaves.

COLOPHON: "20 copies of CASTLE STREET DOGS have been
printed by E. and L. Baskin at the Gehenna Press on Castle St. in
Worcester Massachusetts. August 1952" Colophon signed &
numbered by LB.

TYPE: Goudy Bold; PAPER: Japanese paper, with Atlantic Bond
blanks interleaved.

Sewn into grey boards, with wrappers of Japanese paper, with
CASTLE STREET DOGS in black & pressmark III in red printed
on the front cover.

*Castle Street was short & disreputable, it ended abruptly in Goat's Hill, which had its distinctions in
the mid-nineteenth century. The dilapidated houses were typical of Worcester's three-story row piaz-*

zaed tenements, the people who lived there were lumpenproletarian & the dogs which roamed the street
were filthy & riddled with scurvy & mange. They were scabrous & lousey. I regarded them with care &
interest, drew and made reliefs of them, & fashioned a set of woodengravings which, with a marvelously
apt epigraph by Freud, constitute the content of the book. Two other editions were issued, each with two
additional new woodengravings.

1953

5 · THE TUNNING OF ELYNOUR RUMMYNGE

A POEM CALLED THE TUNNING OF ‖ ELYNOUR RUM-
MYNGE ‖ THE FAMOUS ALE-WIFE OF ENGLAND ‖
WRITTEN BY JOHN SKELTON ‖ POET LAUREAT TO
KING HENRY THE VIII ‖ [3¼-inch rule in red] ‖ THE
GEHENNA PRESS WORCESTER 1953
With 13 wood engravings by LB, printed in various colors.
11½ x 7½. 29 leaves. Printed in red & black.
CONTENTS: 3 blank leaves; (i) blank; (ii) frontispiece: portrait of
Skelton with a rhymed couplet below; (iii) title page; (v) part title,
"HERE AFTER FOLLOWETH THE BOOKE . . ."; 1-34 text &
engravings [pages (4) & (28) are blank]; 1 blank leaf; (37) glossary;
(39) colophon, with pressmark II; (41) pressmark III in red; 2 blank
leaves.
COLOPHON: "118 COPIES OF · THE TUNNING OF
ELYNOUR RUMMYNGE · BY JOHN SKELTON HAVE
BEEN HAND SET AND PRINTED BY ESTHER AND
LEONARD BASKIN AT THE GEHENNA PRESS. THE
TEXT USED IS FROM DYCE'S EDITION OF 1843. THE
ILLUSTRATIONS HAVE BEEN PRINTED FROM THE
WOOD BLOCKS ENGRAVED BY L. BASKIN THIS IS
COPY NO.   " Colophon numbered.
TYPE: text in Artcraft Roman, titling in Forum & Hadriano; PAPER:
Strathmore Text.
The engravings are on pages (ii), (3), 9, 11, 13, (15), 19, 21, 24, (27), 32,
34 & (37). One is reprinted from *Some Engravings By Leonard Baskin*.
Bound in blue paper over boards, with paper labels on the front
cover & spine.

1-page prospectus issued, with a specimen page.

I had begun to teach graphic arts at the Worcester Museum School & somehow convinced the school's director to acquire a rather decrepit but motor-driven platen press & the diverse equipment of a rude printing office. Skelton's wild inebriate verse was hand-set in Artcraft Roman, a hideous face, intended for advertising, cast by Spindler & Bartlett c. 1908 [a cast-off from one of the press' benefactors.] The book's label & its title were printed in Hadriano & Forum, the two typefaces [of capitals only] by Goudy that I can abide; they are, in their use here, typographically unrelated to the book's typeface. The book is the press' first to join image & type on a page. My skills in woodengraving had developed & perhaps that actuality emboldened the printer in pursuit of a greater & sweeter harmony. Lamentably ignorant, I was entirely innocent of the deeper realities of imposition; the pages were singly printed & the binder had to whipstitch them. The book was important for its modest mingling of engraving & type, pointing toward further and greater consorting in later books. The book was given to Bruce Rogers on his eightieth birthday; he responded to it, gesturing and saying, "I like to see an occasional bit of primitive printing."

1954

6· CASTLE STREET DOGS

castle ‖ street ‖ dogs ‖ Wood Engravings By Leonard Baskin [lines 1–3 in red]

Second edition; with 10 engravings, 2 of which are new to this edition.

14¼ x 9¾. 14 leaves. Printed on rectos only.

CONTENTS: (1) title page; (3) quotation from Freud; (5–23) engravings; (25) colophon, with pressmark II in red; (27) pressmark III in red.

COLOPHON: "Twenty-five copies of this, the second edition of Castle Street Dogs have been printed by Esther and Leonard Baskin at the Gehenna Press in South Hadley, Massachusetts. July 1954. This is copy number   " Colophon numbered & signed *Esther & Leonard Baskin* by LB.

One of the new engravings is reprinted from *THE TUNNING OF ELYNOUR RUMMYNGE*.

TYPE: Caslon; PAPER: Troya.

Issued as a single unsewn signature.

7 · BLAKE AND THE YOUTHFUL ANCIENTS

BLAKE AND THE YOUTHFUL ANCIENTS ‖ [2⅛ -inch rule in brown] ‖ BEING PORTRAITS OF WILLIAM BLAKE ‖ AND HIS FOLLOWERS ENGRAVED ON ‖ WOOD BY LEONARD BASKIN ‖ AND WITH A BIOGRAPHICAL ‖ NOTICE BY BENNETT SCHIFF ‖ [2 rows of fleurons in brown] ‖ THE ENTIRE PRINTED ‖ AT THE GEHENNA ‖ PRESS IN NORTH ‖ AMPTON MASS ‖ 1956 ‖ [4 rows of fleurons in brown, forming an inverted triangle]
With 18 wood engravings.

6¾ x 5¾. 45 leaves, untrimmed. Printed in red, brown & black. CONTENTS: 1 blank leaf; (1) title page; (3) quotation from Blake; (5-7) note by Bennett Schiff; (9) part title, "THE PORTRAITS", with 7 rows of fleurons in brown, forming an inverted triangle, below the type; (11–81) engravings & titles; (83) colophon, with pressmark IV in red; 2 blank leaves.

COLOPHON: "FIFTY COPIES OF THIS BOOK HAVE BEEN PRINTED BY ESTHER AND LEONARD BASKIN AT THE GEHENNA PRESS IN NORTHAMPTON MASS. THIS IS COPY NO   " Colophon signed & numbered by LB.

TYPE: Kenntonian; PAPER: Text on Hammer & Anvil, titles on Sekishu, engravings on Mokuroku.

Bound by the Harcourt Bindery in leather & Cockerell marbled paper over boards.

4-page prospectus issued, with an engraving of Blake not used in the book.

This was the last book which was made with my hands, that cessation a benefaction since I was a compositor & pressman of no distinction. This book is an homage to Blake & the dear youths who plied him with honour in his late age. My increased skill in woodengraving is here made manifest & a pattern for a kind of Gehenna Press book makes its beginning here; an introduction succeeded by a series of prints. The title-page reveals the novice's poking into historical sources & exemplars.

THIRTEEN POEMS BY WILFRED OWEN ‖ WITH DRAW-
INGS BY BEN SHAHN ‖ PRINTED AT THE GEHENNA
PRESS ‖ IN NORTHAMPTON MASS MCMLVI [last two
words of lines 1-3, & date in line 4, in red]
With fifteen drawings by Shahn, reproduced by offset, & a portrait
of Owen drawn by Shahn & engraved on boxwood by LB.
13 x 9½. 24 leaves, untrimmed. Printed in red & black.
CONTENTS: 5 blank leaves; (1) half title, with portrait of Owen
above the type; (3) title page; (5) dedication; (6-31) text & drawings;
(33) colophon, with pressmark V in red; (35) pressmark VI in red;
1 blank leaf.
COLOPHON: *"400 copies of this book have been printed by Esther and
Leonard Baskin and Richard Warren at The Gehenna Press: Compositor:
William Scully. Pressman: Romeo Cadieux. The drawings have been
printed by Meriden Gravure. The portrait of Owen was wood engraved by
Leonard Baskin from a drawing by Ben Shahn and printed from the wood
block. Thirty-five copies have been bound in half-leather with an extra
proof of the wood engraving printed on Japanese Vellum, and signed by the
artist and engraver. These copies are numbered I-XXXV. This is copy
number........"* Colophon numbered.
TYPE: Caslon; PAPER: Arnold Ancient Laid.
The entire original edition, not just the *edition de luxe,* was bound
by the Harcourt Bindery in leather & green Fabriano over boards,
& enclosed in a green Fabriano-covered slipcase. A number of unbound copies were later discovered at the Harcourt Bindery, &
were bound in cloth & marbled paper over boards.
4-page prospectus issued, with a specimen page laid in.
Some copies have 5 final blanks, rather than one, after the colophon,
& thus have 28 leaves.

*The four years that stretch between the Elynour Rummynge & the Owen were a time of achievement
become possible & attainment seized. My immense woodcuts were chiefly conceived & cut in those
years, which also saw increased comfort & skill in woodengraving. And beyond the critical intensification
& consolidation of myself as an artist, I began to acquire degrees of knowledge & insight anent printing,*

its history & practice. I began to understand the vast breadth of its limitations, & the rationale of its un-varying custom. Although no books were made, printing, its difficulties and amenities, was never far from my consciousness. My early artistic enterprise was rewarded with a Guggenheim fellowship, an academic appointment at Smith College & a friendship with Ben Shahn, who was the paradigmatic artist, the finder of the means to successfully communicate & express social & political content of an im-mediate & complex nature. He was, I still think, the artist in his era who most compellingly devised the fusing of the physical fabric [form] & political attitudes [content.] I held Shahn in awe, regarded him as a mentor & I managed to escape his stylistic influence. He acceded to my request that he make drawings for a Gehenna edition of a selection of Owen's war execrating poems & he made a beautiful set of drawings which are the chief merit of the book's making. The drawings were photo-lithographically printed with zealous fidelity by the Meriden Gravure Co. under the continuous aegis of Harold Hugo & therefrom began a long & fruitful friendship. The letterpress was printed at The Metcalf Printing & Publishing Co. through the kindness of Richard Warren who had acquired the old printing plant to publish a liberal newspaper in Northampton; his paper failed & he became a printer. In a burst of extraordinary generosi-ty he gave me the key to Metcalf, where I worked at night & weekends. I slowly & inevitably encroached into Metcalf's working time & it was not long before Richard, who had become a friend, became now a partner in Gehenna. I used here a crude & deformed version of Caslon & the overinking & insensible impression testifies to the depth of learning to be acquired.

1957

9 (10) · A LETTER FROM ERNST BARLACH

[engraving] ‖ A LETTER FROM ERNST BARLACH [type in red] Keepsake No. 1. Letter from Barlach to Reinhard Piper, December 28, 1911. With three woodengraved portraits of Barlach by LB. 6 x 4½. 8 leaves, untrimmed. Printed in red & black.

CONTENTS: 1 blank leaf; (1) title page; (3-7) text; (8) 2 engravings; (9-10) text; (11) colophon; 1 blank leaf.

COLOPHON: "150 COPIES OF THIS KEEPSAKE WERE PRINTED BY ESTHER & LEONARD BASKIN AT THE GEHENNA PRESS IN NORTHAMPTON MASSACH-USETTS 26 MARCH MCMLVII"

TYPE: Kenntonian; PAPER: Linweave Text, Hammer & Anvil, Flemish Laid or Warren's [some copies on each.]
Some copies bound by the Harcourt Bindery in leather & Cockerell marbled paper over boards; these copies have an addi-tional 16 final blanks. The rest were sewn into grey boards, with wrappers of decorated paper, & a paper label on the front cover.

10 (9) · RIDDLE POEMS

RIDDLE POEMS ‖ [4 fleurons in red] ‖ *EMILY DICKINSON* ‖
THE GEHENNA PRESS ‖ 1957
6¼ x 5¼. 24 leaves, untrimmed. Printed in red & black.
CONTENTS: 2 blank leaves; (1) title page; (3) dedication; (5-34) 15 rid-
dle poems in frames of typographic ornaments [on rectos] & solu-
tions [on versos]; 1 blank leaf; (37) colophon, with pressmark IV in
red & V in black; (39) pressmark VI in red; 2 blank leaves.
COLOPHON: "TWO HUNDRED COPIES OF THIS BOOK
HAVE BEEN PRINTED BY ESTHER & LEONARD BASKIN
& RICHARD WARREN AT THE GEHENNA PRESS IN
NORTHAMPTON MASSACHUSETTS THIS IS COPY
NO.   " Copyright notice follows. Colophon numbered &
signed *Esther & Leonard Baskin* by LB.
TYPE: Caslon; PAPER: Venezia.
Bound by the Harcourt Bindery. 175 copies bound in green
Japanese paper over boards, with paper labels on the front cover
& spine. 25 copies, numbered I-XXV, bound in leather & the
same Japanese paper over boards.
4-page prospectus issued.

11 · VOYAGES

VOYAGES SIX POEMS FROM WHITE BUILDINGS ‖ BY
HART CRANE WITH WOOD ENGRAVINGS BY ‖
LEONARD BASKIN PUBLISHED BY THE MUSEUM ‖ OF
MODERN ART NEW YORK CITY MCMLVII [first word of
line 1, & date in line 4, in red; engraving to the left of the type]
With 6 wood engravings & one woodcut, printed in various
colors.
9½ x 11, oblong. 16 leaves, untrimmed. Printed in red, green &
black.
CONTENTS: 1 blank leaf; (1) half title; (3) title page; (5) engraving on
Mending Tissue; (7-10) text, with an engraving on (9); (11) moun-
ted woodcut on green Moriki; (12-13) text; (14-15) mounted 2-page

engraving on Mending Tissue; (16-18) text, with an engraving
on (17); (19-20) engraving printed on both sides of a sheet of
Mending Tissue; (21) text; (23) colophon; (25) pressmark VII in red;
2 blank leaves.

COLOPHON: "This book, the second of a series of limited editions
published by The Museum of Modern Art under the direction of
Monroe Wheeler has been designed, illustrated and printed by
Leonard Baskin at The Gehenna Press, Northampton, Mass. in
November 1957. The poems have been reprinted by permission of
the Liveright Publishing Corporation from "Collected Poems of
Hart Crane." The Perpetua type has been set by hand. The illustrations have been printed from six original boxwood engravings and
one cherry woodcut on Amalfi Italian hand-made paper and on
Moriki and Mending Tissue, both hand-made in Japan. The edition
is limited to 975 numbered copies and 25 lettered review copies, all
all signed by Mr. Baskin. this is copy number   " Colophon signed &
numbered by LB.
Sewn into blue wrappers with a paper label on the front cover, &
laid into a portfolio of blue paper over boards, with paper labels on
the front cover & spine.
4-page prospectus issued.

*A terribly overcomplicated book, its vagaries in structure & its bizarreries of sequence reveal far more
about my struggles with typography & woodengraving than about Crane. The book wants coherence,
strength & order but it does startle & somewhat dazzle as it falls apart. Sometime during 1958, Alex
Page, then professor at the University of Massachusetts, brought a colleague to our house & an intense
argument about 'Moby Dick' blew-up, but Sidney Kaplan was able to so overwhelmingly quote chapter
& verse that he swept all before him & that formidable erudition couched within his ready friendliness
formed the basis of our enduring friendship. He had long been involved with printing & had planned
with his father-in-law, a jobbing printer in Astoria, N.Y., & a friend to print a work of Schopenhauer in
the austere & splendid manner of Willy Wiegand & the Bremer Press, whose prospectuses they
received. Sidney Kaplan came in time to be a vital & crucial member of the small Gehenna circle. His
polymathic presence was continuously instructive, & his influence was enormous & whatever textual
contribution the press has made is due to his efforts: he was the editor of the press.*

An ‖ ABC ‖ *with* ‖ *best wishes for 1958* ‖ *from* ‖ *Esther & Leonard Baskin* ‖ [small engraving] [lines 2 & 6 in red]
Keepsake No. 2.
4¾ x 5¼, oblong. 32 leaves. Printed in red & black.
CONTENTS: 2 blank leaves; (1) title page; (4-55) text; (57) colophon; 1 blank leaf.
COLOPHON: "500 copies have been printed at the Gehenna Press in Northampton, Mass. The illustrations for letters G R T V and X have been printed from the original blocks engraved by Thomas Bewick. Those for B N and Q are from 19th Century wood-engravings. A and D are from blocks engraved by L.B. The rest are from 19th Century stereotypes."
TYPE: Caslon & Wood Type; PAPER: Strathmore Text.
Stapled into purple Montgolfier wrappers, with ABC printed on the front & back covers.
Some copies substitute *Marian & Dick Warren* for *Esther & Leonard Baskin* on line 6 of the title page; other copies omit line 6 entirely.

1958

13 (14) · PREDATORY BIRDS

PREDATORY BIRDS ‖ TEN LITHOGRAPHS BY ‖ AUBREY SCHWARTZ ‖ WITH A POEM BY ‖ ANTHONY HECHT ‖ THE GEHENNA PRESS ‖ 1958 [first & last lines in red]
30 x 22½. 13 sheets, untrimmed. Printed on rectos only in red & black.
CONTENTS: (1) title page; (2) text; (3-12) lithographs; (13) colophon, with pressmark IX in red.
COLOPHON: *"Twenty-five copies of this portfolio have been issued by the Gehenna Press in January 1958. The lithographs have been printed from the stones at Robert Blackburn's Graphic Workshop, New York City; the letterpress in Northampton, Massachusetts. The paper is handmade Arches. This is copy number* "Colophon numbered.
TYPE: Caslon.
Laid into a portfolio with two ribbon ties & a paper label on the front cover.

HORNED BEETLES AND OTHER INSECTS ‖ [2⅞-inch rule in red] ‖ ETCHINGS BY LEONARD BASKIN ‖ THE GEHENNA PRESS ‖ NORTHAMPTON ‖ MCMLVIII
With 34 etchings, printed in various colors.
6½ x 10, oblong. 75 leaves, untrimmed. Printed on rectos only in red & black.
CONTENTS: 4 blank leaves; (1) title page; (3) quotation from Darwin; (5-131) etchings & titles; (133) colophon, with pressmark VIII; 4 blank leaves.
COLOPHON: "THIRTY COPIES OF THIS BOOK HAVE BEEN PRINTED AT THE GEHENNA PRESS, NORTH-AMPTON, MASSACHUSETTS. THE ETCHINGS HAVE BEEN PRINTED FROM THE PLATES BY THE ARTIST WITH THE ASSISTANCE OF LOUIS SMITH, ON A VAR-IETY OF EUROPEAN AND JAPANESE HAND-MADE PAPERS. THIS IS COPY NO........" Colophon signed & numbered by LB.
TYPE: Kenntonian; PAPER: various English, French, Italian & Japanese hand-made papers, & some early Nineteenth Century Swiss papers.
Bound by the Harcourt Bindery in full leather, & enclosed in a linen-covered slipcase.
4-page prospectus issued.
In copies 1-5, some of the etchings are touched; these copies are accompanied by an original drawing by LB.

The summer of 1958 was spent printing the etchings for "Horned Beetles & Other Insects", the first Gehenna Press book to use etchings. Because the insects were pictured in realistic & fantastic guises, I decided to put the creatures' Latin names on the inter-leaving tissues. It was at that moment that the crucial intervention of Harold McGrath occurred. He was a pressman at Metcalf & Richard Warren assigned him the task of printing those names in red & thus began the ensuing & fruitful relationship. McGrath & I in tandem made an interactive & productive team. His was the perfected means to carry out my printing needs & typographic fantasies. He had the infinite patience of the immaculate compositor & in his press-work he built ever more & more complex & intricate make-readies to assure perfect and even impression tone. He possessed the quotient of excessive staying power that suberb presswork re-

quires. Without McGrath 'Flosculi Sententiarum' would hardly have been, then & there, possible, nor many another effect that bespeak the look & feel of Gehenna Press books. It did not take very long for Harold McGrath to become a full-time employee of a more formally organized Gehenna Press. I used to boastfully prattle that the Gehenna Press was the only private press with a full-time employee. It was an untenable proposition for it ensured that McGrath would inevitably be idle for long periods, which indeed he was. It was distressful to McGrath & economically idiotic for the press. The lead-time as it is called between the conception of a book & its actual execution is long, arduous & consumptive of time. But its financial loss was perhaps more than made-up by the press' serving & functioning as a free academy of the typographic arts. Apprentices were always welcome & Harold McGrath's great patience was further tried as he slowly & skillfully taught the young people the mysteries of composition & printing techniques. That the Gehenna Press served as a fountainhead for a generation of bookworkers significantly adds to the totality of its achievements.

15 · THE SEVEN DEADLY SINS

THE SEVEN DEADLY SINS POEMS BY ‖ ANTHONY HECHT WOOD ENGRAVINGS ‖ BY LEONARD BASKIN THE GEHENNA ‖PRESS NORTHAMPTON MASSACH-USETTS ‖ 1958 [first 4 words of line 1, last 2 words of line 3 & first word of line 4 in red]

With 7 wood engravings.

7⅝ x 7¾, oblong. 12 leaves, untrimmed. Printed on rectos only in red & black.

CONTENTS: 1 blank leaf; (1) title page; (3) blank, with an erratum slip pasted in; (5-17) text & engravings; (19) colophon, with pressmarks V & VII in red; 1 blank leaf.

COLOPHON: "Three hundred copies of this book have been printed at the Gehenna Press in Northampton, Mass. The engravings have been printed from the original blocks. This is copy   "
Colophon signed & numbered by LB, & signed by Hecht.

TYPE: Perpetua; PAPER: Mokuroku.

100 copies bound in cloth & paper over boards, with a leather label on the spine; 200 copies sewn into blue wrappers, with a paper label on the front cover.

4-page prospectus issued.

There was a second printing, identical to the first except for the following: (1) there is no erratum slip; (2) the colophon reads

"Three hundred copies of the second printing of this book . . ."; (3) all 300 copies were stapled into blue wrappers, with a paper label on the front cover.

I was, by 1958, deep in enchanted pursuit of early emblem books. A new friendship was wrought with the splendid poet Anthony Hecht, & given his great interest in formal poetics, a new emblem book inevitably resulted; it is entirely conceived in sixteenth century modalities. The earlier emblem books combined three often quite disparate elements, forcing from this yoking of dissimilars new meanings. A motto would be joined to an image & to a poem or a bit of prose, & when understood together, they yielded up the concept. This easily developed into a humanist plaything with arcana and bizarrerie, their books replete with enigma & secrecy. 'The Seven Deadly Sins' is without mystification, its emblematic intentions are crystal clear.

16 · A HOUSE TO BE BORN IN

A House To Be Born In ‖ [4 fleurons in red] ‖ JAY LEYDA ‖ Wood Engraving by ‖ GEORGE LOCKWOOD ‖ [2 fleurons in red] ‖ THE GEHENNA PRESS ‖ 1958 ‖ [1 fleuron in red]
9¼ x 7½. 12 leaves. Printed in red & black.
CONTENTS: 2 blank leaves; (1) title page; (3) engraving on tissue; (5-10) text; 1 blank leaf; 1 blank tissue leaf; (15) colophon, with pressmarks IV & V in red; 2 blank leaves.
COLOPHON: "ONE HUNDRED COPIES OF THIS BOOK HAVE BEEN PRINTED FOR JAY LEYDA AT THE GEHENNA PRESS, NORTHAMPTON, MASS. THE WOOD ENGRAVING IS BY GEORGE LOCKWOOD. This is Copy No........" Colophon signed & numbered by Lockwood.
TYPE: Kenntonian; PAPER: Warren's Olde Style & tissue.
Stapled into blue wrappers, with a paper label on the front cover.

17 · STRUWWELPETER

STRUWWELPETER ‖ A POEM BY ‖ ANTHONY HECHT [first line in red]
Keepsake No. 3. With 4 wood engravings by LB, including the one on the front cover.
4¼ x 3¾. 10 leaves. Printed in red & black.
CONTENTS: 1 blank leaf; (1) "*With wishes for a happy* ‖ *1959* ‖ *The Gehenna Press*"; (3) title page; (5) engraving; (7-12) text, with

engravings on (8) & (11); (13) colophon; 2 blank leaves.
COLOPHON: "400 copies printed at The Gehenna Press, Northampton, Mass. The wood engravings have been printed from the
blocks engraved by L.B."
TYPE: Garamond; PAPER: Warren's Olde Style & Japanese tissue.
Stapled into wrappers, with STRUWWELPETER in red & a
wood engraving in black printed on the front cover.
Some copies substitute *Marian and Richard Warren* or *Esther and
Leonard Baskin* for *The Gehenna Press* on line 3 of page (1), & some
omit line 3 entirely. Some copies omit STRUWWELPETER &
have an earlier state of the wood engraving on the front cover.

1959
18 · HOMAGE TO REDON
HOMAGE TO REDON ‖ TEN PORTRAITS ‖ CUT &
ENGRAVED ON WOOD ‖ BY ‖ GEORGE LOCKWOOD ‖
WITH ‖ REDON'S ESSAY ‖ ON BRESDIN LITHOGRAPHY
AND ‖ THE NATURE OF BLACK ‖ TRANSLATED ‖ BY
HYMAN SWETZOFF ‖ THE ‖ GEHENNA PRESS ‖
MCMLIX [first line in red]
With 10 woodcut & wood engraved portraits, printed in various
colors.
11 x 9. 34 leaves, untrimmed.
CONTENTS: 2 blank leaves; (1) title page; (3) engraving tipped-on;
(5-19) text; 1 blank tissue leaf; (23-55) engravings & woodcuts;
1 blank tissue leaf; (59) colophon, with pressmarks IV & VII in red
& V in brown; 2 blank leaves.
COLOPHON: "One hundred and fifty copies of this book have been
printed at The Gehenna Press in Northampton, Massachusetts.
The portraits have been printed from the blocks on a variety of
Japanese hand-made papers. This is copy number   Finished
January 27, 1959" Colophon numbered.
TYPE: Caslon; PAPER: text on Millbourne Book Laid.
Bound by the Harcourt Bindery in leather & Ingres d'Arches over

boards, & enclosed in a slipcase covered with the same paper.
4-page prospectus issued.
10 copies numbered I–X are accompanied by an original drawing
by Lockwood.

I was more interested in Bresdin than in his student Redon, but I liked this oddment of a lecture, which the innovative Boston art dealer Hyman Swetzoff had translated. The printing of this text provided an opportunity for my friend and then Smith College colleague, George Lockwood, to make a set of woodengravings & woodcuts in homage to Redon, the master he most admired. The woodengraving of Redon in profile, embedded in flowers, is printed from five blocks & is very beautiful. The Caslon type used here is classic & disposed as intended, clearly & sharply printed.

19 (22) · WITH SANDY WE HAVE TROUBLES
WITH SANDY ‖ WE HAVE TROUBLES ‖ [2½-inch rule in brown] ‖ *Compiled in Loving Memory* ‖ *of* ‖ *Sophie Page* ‖ *the Gentle Mistress of a Dog Named Sandy* ‖ *for her* ‖ *Family & Friends* ‖ *by* ‖ *Alex Page* ‖ PRIVATELY PRINTED ‖ 1959
7 x 5½. 10 leaves.
CONTENTS: 1 blank leaf; (1) blank; (2) mounted photograph; (3) title page; (5) note on text; (7–14) text; (15) colophon; 1 blank leaf.
COLOPHON: "100 COPIES HAVE BEEN PRINTED FOR ALEX PAGE AT THE GEHENNA PRESS IN NORTHAMPTON, MASSACHUSETTS"
TYPE: Garamond; PAPER: Ticonderoga Text & Flemish.
Stapled into blue wrappers, with a paper label on the front cover.

20 (19) · OF GARDENS
OF GARDENS ‖ *FRANCIS BACON* [type within line cut of a drawing of a floral wreath by LB, in green]
Text pages framed by rules in green.
6 x 4½. 12 leaves, untrimmed. Printed in italic, in orange & black.
CONTENTS: 1 blank leaf; (1) title page; (3–19) text; (21) colophon, with pressmark X in orange.
COLOPHON: *"TWO HUNDRED COPIES OF THIS BOOK HAVE BEEN PRINTED ON MILLBOURN BOOK LAID BY ESTHER AND LEONARD BASKIN AND RICHARD*

WARREN AT THE GEHENNA PRESS IN NORTHAMP-TON, MASSACHUSETTS. THE BOOK HAS BEEN SET IN INTERTYPE GARAMOND. HAROLD McGRATH WAS THE PRESSMAN. PRINTING WAS COMPLETED IN MARCH, 1959. THIS IS NUMBER ''Colophon numbered. In many copies, the colophon is signed by Esther or Leonard Baskin.

Sewn into thin boards covered with Japanese decorated paper, with a paper label on the front cover.

4-page prospectus issued.

21 (20) · AUGURIES OF INNOCENCE

AUGURIES OF INNOCENCE ‖ BY ‖ WILLIAM BLAKE ‖ WOOD ENGRAVINGS ‖ BY ‖ LEONARD BASKIN ‖ PRINTED ‖ FOR ‖ THE PRINT CLUB ‖ OF ‖ PHILADEL-PHIA ‖ AT THE ‖ GEHENNA PRESS ‖ 1959 [type within an arrangement of horizontal & vertical rules in red]

With 8 wood engravings.

9¼ x 5¾. 10 leaves, untrimmed. Printed in red & black.

CONTENTS: 1 blank leaf; (1) title page; (3) portrait of Blake; (4-11) text & engravings; (13) colophon; (15) pressmark XI; 1 blank leaf.

COLOPHON: "250 COPIES OF THIS BOOK HAVE BEEN PRINTED FOR THE PRINT CLUB OF PHILADELPHIA BY ESTHER & LEONARD BASKIN & RICHARD WARREN AT THE GEHENNA PRESS IN NORTHAMPTON, MASSACH-USETTS. THE ENGRAVINGS HAVE BEEN PRINTED FROM THE BLOCKS. THE BOOK WAS PRINTED ON AMALFI, AN ITALIAN HAND-MADE PAPER IN MONO-TYPE BEMBO. HAROLD MCGRATH WAS THE PRESS-MAN. THIS IS COPY NUMBER '' Colophon signed & numbered by LB.

PAPER: initial & final blanks are Japanese tissue.

Sewn into grey Fabriano wrappers, with a paper label on the front cover. 100 copies were available from the Gehenna Press, of which

40 were laid into a portfolio of leather & grey Fabriano over boards, with an additional set of the engravings on Japanese vellum, each one signed by LB.

In 1968 Grossman Publishers, New York, issued a trade edition of the book, including 100 copies bound in quarter-leather, with an impression of one of the engravings printed from the block.

This more mature printed tribute to William Blake was commissioned by 'The Print Club of Philadelphia' & in it I begin to invent typographic structures of originality & sensitivity. Nothing grand or stunning but spaces spread & contained with a just nicety & rules deployed with grace & subtlety & bits of color judiciously used. There is a newer sensibility in type choice, its sizes in relation to the book's eight woodengravings. The binding in its easy simplicity is expressive of deepening understanding. This is a crucial book in the growth of the printer's typographic insight & it bespeaks enlarged prospects as to the controlling & marshalling the necessities & inevitabilities in the making & ordering of books. It was through Auguries that I became acquainted with, & later the friend of, Seymour Adelman, then president of the Philadelphia print club, an incredible collector & a remarkable person.

22 (21) · CASTLE STREET DOGS

[engraving in orange] ‖ CASTLE STREET DOGS ‖ WOOD-ENGRAVINGS BY LEONARD BASKIN ‖ THE GEHENNA PRESS ‖ 1959

Third edition; with 12 engravings, 2 of which are new to this edition.

9¼ x 6¼. 14 sheets, untrimmed. Printed on rectos only.

CONTENTS: (1) title page; (2) quotation from Freud; (3-13) engravings; (14) colophon, with pressmark VII.

COLOPHON: "100 copies of this the third and final edition of Castle Street Dogs have been printed at the Gehenna Press in Northampton, Massachusetts. Two new dogs have been added and they as well as the others have been printed from blocks. The paper is Mokuroko [sic], hand-made in Japan. Number   " Colophon signed & numbered by LB.

TYPE: Perpetua.

Issued in sheets, laid into purple wrappers, with a paper label on the front cover.

1960

23 · ERNST BARLACH

ERNST BARLACH ‖ [engraving] ‖ TWO ACTS FROM ‖
THE FLOOD ‖ A LETTER ON KANDINSKY ‖ EIGHT
SCULPTURES ‖ BRECHT ‖ *NOTES ON THE BARLACH
EXHIBITION* ‖ NORTHAMPTON ‖ MCMLX [first & last
lines in red]
With a wood engraving by LB.
9 x 6. 26 leaves. Printed in red & black.
CONTENTS: I blank leaf; (1) title page; (2) biographical note; 3–32 text
of acts II & V of *The Flood;* 4 leaves of photographs; 33–34 letter from
Barlach on Kandinsky; 35–39 Brecht's *Notes on the Barlach Exhibi-
tion;* (40) colophon, with pressmark II in red; 1 blank leaf.
COLOPHON: "This insert was printed at The Gehenna Press for
The Massachusetts Review. The wood engraved portrait by Leonard
Baskin was printed from the block. The plates of Barlach's sculp-
ture were printed at The Meriden Gravure Company. The photo-
graphs were supplied by R. Piper Verlag."
TYPE: Caslon & Perpetua; PAPER: blue Ticonderoga Text.
The engraving is reprinted from *A LETTER FROM ERNST
BARLACH.*
A few copies were bound in brown wrappers, with ERNST
BARLACH in a box of rules printed on the front cover. Most were
bound into the Spring 1960 *Massachusetts Review;* these copies have
only 24 leaves, since the blanks are omitted.

24 · A LETTER FROM GUSTAVE FLAUBERT

A LETTER FROM GUSTAVE FLAUBERT ‖ [engraving] [type
in red]
Keepsake No. 4. Letter from Flaubert to Maxime Du Camp, June
19, 1852. With a wood engraving by LB.
6 x 4½. 8 leaves, untrimmed. Printed in red & black.
CONTENTS: I blank leaf; (1) title page; (3–9) text; (11)colophon, with
pressmark XII; (13) pressmark XI.

COLOPHON: "300 copies of this keepsake were printed at the Gehenna Press in Northampton Massachusetts by Esther & Leonard Baskin & Richard Warren for the Friends & Patrons of the press. The translation is by Francis Steegmuller & the copyright is held by Farrar, Straus & Young who have given their permission for its reprinting here. The wood engraving has been engraved by L.B. & has been printed from the block. 7 May MCMLX"
TYPE: Garamond; PAPER: Mokuroku.
Sewn into grey Fabriano wrappers, with a yellow paper label on the front cover.

25 · THE MIDGET & THE DWARF
THE MIDGET & THE DWARF ‖ TEN LITHOGRAPHS BY ‖ AUBREY SCHWARTZ ‖ MCMLX
30 x 22 ½. 12 sheets, untrimmed. Printed on rectos only.
CONTENTS: (1) title page; (2-11) lithographs; (12) colophon.
COLOPHON: *"This portfolio of ten lithographs was printed from stone by Garo Antreasian at Tamarind Lithography Workshop, Los Angeles, in an edition of twenty numbered impressions and five artist's proofs on Arches paper, plus nine Tamarind Impressions on Rives BFK paper. Some trial proofs exist which are records at Tamarind. Binding by Margaret Lecky. Letterpress by the Gehenna Press, Northampton, Massachusetts. This is number   "* Colophon signed & numbered by Schwartz.
TYPE: Caslon.
Laid into a buckram portfolio.

1961
26 (25) · EULOGY FOR HYMAN RATNER
EULOGY FOR HYMAN RATNER
By Saul H. Fisher.
9 x 6. 6 leaves, untrimmed.
CONTENTS: 1 blank leaf; (1) title page; (3-6) text; (7) colophon; 1 blank leaf.
COLOPHON: "ONE HUNDRED COPIES PRINTED AT THE

GEHENNA PRESS NORTHAMPTON MCMLXI"
TYPE: Palatino; PAPER: Amalfi.
Sewn into grey wrappers, with EULOGY FOR HYMAN
RATNER printed on the front cover.

27 (26) · THE WOOD ENGRAVINGS OF LEONARD BASKIN
THE WOOD ENGRAVINGS OF ‖ LEONARD BASKIN ‖
1948-1959 ‖ IMPRESSIONS FROM THE BLOCKS ‖ PRIN-
TED AT ‖ THE GEHENNA PRESS ‖ NORTHAMPTON ‖
1961 [lines 3 & 6 in red]
With 188 wood engravings, printed in various colors. Each
engraving is numbered, the numbers printed blind. "In some
cases...type reproduc[es] the original function as ex-libris,
press mark, etc." [from the prospectus.]
17 x 17½, oblong. 74 sheets, untrimmed. Printed on rectos only in
red & black.
CONTENTS: (1) title page; (2-6) catalogue & index; (7-73) engravings; (74) colophon, with pressmark XIIIa in red.
COLOPHON: "TWENTY-FOUR COPIES PRINTED AT THE
GEHENNA PRESS IN NORTHAMPTON MASSACHUS-
ETTS THE WORK FINISHED DURING THE MONTH OF
MARCH MCMLXI THIS IS COPY   " Colophon signed &
numbered by LB.
TYPE: Palatino; PAPER: engravings on Mokuroku & others, text on
Umbria.
Many of the engravings are reprinted from earlier Gehenna Press
books.
Laid into a buckram-covered portfolio, and enclosed in a leather &
marbled paper slipcase.
4-page prospectus issued.

*I cannot remember the impetus that drove me to collect all of my woodengravings into this large & severe-
ly limited book. Was it an instinctive insight that woodengraving as a medium was nearing its end for
me? Actually, twenty-two others appeared in later Gehenna books. The thrust of my engraving in end-
grain boxwood had been sapped. Why? There are manifold difficulties inherent in woodengraving. It is
technically the most demanding of the graphic media & a very long time is required to make accommoda-*

tion to its specificities. To achieve comfort & ease in handling the burin, to overcome its handle's ungainly insistence on pushing deep into & against the fatty palm with the fingers splayed along the tool's shaft, takes at least one year. It is an odd palmy embrace & time must be contained by patience for naturalness & skill to develop in deploying the tools. A sorry tradition developed, derived from Bewick, which became epidemic & robbed much of woodengraving of its lustre. The dim practitioners see the block as a field of black in which the sharp pointed tools pick-out whites & a design is revealed. The arrant difficulties of the medium precluded the involvement of major artists & the monotonous, feeble & pallid prints that the very skilled hands of very minor artists produced, desperately want a rich black line crackling & snapping its way across white space. The blunder is vested in allowing a pre-conceived idea of what a woodengraving must look like. Models that belie this limiting vision are plentiful: see the rare best of Doré in his wild & extravagant inventions for Balzac's 'Droll Stories' or Daumier's for 'Nemesis Medical' or Menzel's for 'Frederick the Great.' The point is that the crucial life of the woodengraving is its extraordinary capacity to transform a drawing into a new & palpable actuality. There is a metamorphosing factor in the drawing so easily & readily onto the block & then the necessity to dig the design out of the metal-like hardness of the wood. It is a particular intensity that derives from the rendering of the fluid & flowing through means that are halting, static & intractable. The other difficulty intrinsic to woodengraving derives from the committed engagement required, the endless hours of application to what I here denominate as true woodengraving. The virtuosic skills demanded, the eye-wearying, the brain-draining, the hand-aching are all difficult to sustain. But perhaps even more difficult is the curling-in on oneself that long stands of woodengraving induce: the trenchant attention to the area of engraving, the constant pertinence, the peering through magnification, tend in the aggregate to isolate the engraver. And those myriads & tangles & mazes of lines, the dense confluence of tonalities & textures all prove in the end a dazzlement, a blandishment, a diminishment. What is needed is a brain clarifying gesture that is freer, larger, unconstrained & a release from the restrictive demands of woodengraving. Both etching & lithography are free-form in comparison & they as media are both capable of a large compass & of smaller refinements & can probe reality with near endless variation.

28 (27) · TEN WOODCUTS

LEONARD BASKIN ‖ [4⅛-inch rule in red] ‖ TEN WOOD-CUTS ‖ R M LIGHT AND COMPANY ‖ 421 BEACON ST BOSTON 15 MASSACHUSETTS

Catalogue of 10 woodcuts offered for sale. With reproductions of the woodcuts, reduced & printed from line cuts.

13 x 10. 10 leaves, untrimmed. Printed in red & black.

CONTENTS: (1) title page; (3) note by LB; (5–14) woodcuts; (15) biographical note on LB & dealer's note; 1 blank stub; (19) colophon.

COLOPHON: "FIFTEEN HUNDRED COPIES PRINTED FOR R.M. LIGHT & CO., AT THE GEHENNA PRESS IN

NORTHAMPTON MASSACHUSETTS APRIL 1961"
TYPE: Perpetua & Garamond; PAPER: Frankfurt.
Sewn into blue wrappers, with LEONARD BASKIN TEN
WOODCUTS in a box of rules printed on the front cover.

1962
29 (30) · FOUR PORTRAIT BUSTS BY FRANCESCO LAURANA
FOUR PORTRAIT BUSTS BY FRANCESCO LAURANA ‖
PHOTOGRAPHS BY CLARENCE KENNEDY WITH AN ‖
INTRODUCTORY BIOGRAPHICAL ESSAY BY RUTH ‖
WEDGWOOD KENNEDY · THE GEHENNA PRESS
[fleuron in red] ‖ MCMLXII [first & last lines in red]
Gehenna Essays in Art, No. 1.
9¾ x 7¼. 34 leaves, untrimmed. Printed in red & black.
CONTENTS: 1 blank leaf; (1) series title; (3) title page; (5) dedication;
(7-29) text; (31) part title, "PLATES"; (32-55) plates & captions;
(57) part title, "BIBLIOGRAPHY"; (58-59) bibliography; (61) col-
ophon, with pressmark XI; 2 blank leaves.
COLOPHON: "Five hundred copies of this the first volume in the
Gehenna Essays in Art have been printed at the Gehenna Press in
Northampton, Massachusetts. The pressman was Harold
McGrath. The plates have been printed at the Meriden Gravure
Co., in Meriden, Connecticut. The text has been set in monotype
Centaur and Arrighi types and printed on Amalfi, a handmade
Italian paper; the plates on Tovil handmade in England. Fifty
copies have been specially bound at the Harcourt Bindery in one-
half oasis niger and are lettered I-L This is copy number   ″
Colophon numbered.
Regular edition bound by Russell-Rutter Co. in grey Roma over
boards, with an imitation vellum spine. Copies I-L bound in
leather & the same Roma over boards, with an extra suite of the
plates printed on shizuoka vellum wrapped in a sheet of Roma, &
the whole enclosed in a slipcase covered with the same paper.
4-page prospectus issued, with a sample plate laid in.

There is very little serious writing anent aspects of painting, sculpture & engraving that is not art-historical & essentially unreadable. The Gehenna Essays in Art was a real but failed attempt to find remedial texts with an abundance of faithful reproductions. The causes of the series' failure are twofold: 1, The belle-lettristic style was not, it developed, available to our writers; & 2, many promised texts were not delivered. The reproductions of Clarence Kennedy's beautiful & unfailingly revelatory photographs were printed by Harold Hugo at the Meriden Gravure Co., who acted as a silent partner in this enterprise. The English hand-made paper, which I insisted on, tended to pick, that is, its fibers left tiny white streaks on the surface of the print. To overcome this blight, blocks of lacquer the size of the reproduced photograph were printed, which contained the fibers but also deepened & enriched the three hundred-line offsetting. The plates resemble, because of the lacquer's profound effect, the finest collotype printing.

30 (31) · OF GARLANDS AND CORONARY

OF ‖ GARLANDS ‖ AND CORONARY ‖ OR GARLAND ‖ PLANTS ‖ THOMAS BROWNE ‖ TO ‖ JOHN EVELYN ‖ ESQ · F · R · S [line 6 in red; all type within a line cut of a wreath in green]

Keepsake No. 5. The text of the colophon is printed within a line cut of a different wreath, also in green.

9 x 6. 8 leaves, untrimmed. Printed in red, green & black.

CONTENTS: 1 blank leaf; (1) title page; (3–8) text; (9) colophon; 2 blank leaves.

COLOPHON: "OF THIS KEEPSAKE 500 COPIES HAVE BEEN PRINTED FOR THE SMITH COLLEGE MUSEUM OF ART AT THE GEHENNA PRESS IN NORTHAMPTON MASSACHETTS MCMLXII"

TYPE: Bembo; PAPER: Millbourn Book Laid.

Sewn into grey Fabriano wrappers with the type from the title page, arranged in the same way but within a third line cut of a wreath in green, printed on the front cover.

250 additional copies were printed; they have the following notice, printed in Perpetua, mounted on the initial blank: "The Gehenna Press The Smith College Museum of Art has permitted us to overprint 250 copies of this keepsake. We send it in expression of gratitude for the patience of our patrons and the loyalty of our friends."

31 (28) · FIFTEEN WOODCUTS

FIFTEEN WOODCUTS ‖ [5-inch rule in red] ‖ LEONARD
BASKIN ‖ THE FRIENDS OF ART ‖ BOSTON UNIVER-
SITY ‖ 1962 [date in red]

With one wood engraving, printed from the block, and reproductions of 15 woodcuts, printed by offset.

22 x 16. 18 sheets. Printed on rectos only in red & black.

CONTENTS: (1) title page; (2) colophon, with pressmark XIIIb in
red; (3) wood engraving, *Bartleby the Scrivener,* with "PRINTED
FROM THE BLOCK AT THE GEHENNA PRESS" in red
below; (4-18) woodcuts.

COLOPHON: "500 COPIES OF THIS PORTFOLIO HAVE
BEEN PRINTED ON STONERIDGE TEXT. THE REPRO-
DUCTIONS WERE PRINTED BY THE MERIDEN GRAV-
URE COMPANY. LETTERPRESS BY THE GEHENNA
PRESS. 100 COPIES NUMBERED I-C ARE ACCOMPANIED
BY AN ORIGINAL WOODCUT PRINTED FROM THE
BLOCK. THIS IS COPY   " Colophon signed & numbered
by LB.

TYPE: Bembo.

Laid into a linen-covered portfolio, with a paper label on the front
cover.

Copies I-C have a woodcut, *Jan Lievens,* printed from the block on
Japanese paper, between (2) & (3), and thus have 19 sheets, not 18.

32 (29) · DRAWINGS FOR THE ILIAD

DRAWINGS ‖ FOR THE ‖ ILIAD ‖ LEONARD BASKIN ‖
1962 [lines 3 & 5 in red]

With 60 drawings, reproduced by offset, & 3 etchings, signed &
numbered, by LB.

26 ¼ x 20. 69 sheets, untrimmed. Printed on rectos only in red &
black.

CONTENTS: (i) blank; (ii) title page; (iii-v) list of drawings;
(vi-viii) etchings; 1-60 drawings; (61) colophon, with pressmark

XIIIb in red.

COLOPHON: "150 COPIES OF DRAWINGS FOR THE ILIAD
HAVE BEEN PUBLISHED BY DELPHIC ARTS OF NEW
YORK CITY. THE PAPER THROUGHOUT IS FABRIANO.
THE DRAWINGS HAVE BEEN REPRODUCED BY THE
MERIDEN GRAVURE COMPANY, THE TEXT MATTER
PRINTED AT THE GEHENNA PRESS. THE QUOTA-
TIONS ARE USED WITH THE PERMISSION OF THE
UNIVERSITY OF CHICAGO PRESS WHO HOLD THE
COPYRIGHT FOR LATTIMORE'S TRANSLATION OF
THE ILIAD. THE EDITION HAS BEEN ARRANGED AS
FOLLOWS. COPIES NUMBER ONE THROUGH NINETY
ARE ACCOMPANIED BY THREE ORIGINAL ETCHINGS
BY LEONARD BASKIN. COPIES NUMBERED I-LX
HAVE AN EXTRA SUITE OF THE ETCHINGS PRINTED
ON JAPAN NACRE AND ARE ACCOMPANIED BY AN
ORIGINAL DRAWING. THE WORK COMPLETED IN
OCTOBER MCMLXII. THIS IS COPY   " Colophon signed
& numbered by LB.

TYPE: Bembo.

Copies I-LX laid into a portfolio of leather & coarse linen over
boards with cloth ties, & copies 1-90 into one of coarse linen over
boards with cloth ties, all by the Harcourt Bindery.

4-page prospectus issued.

These drawings were commissioned by the University of Chicago
Press, & 49 of them appeared in an edition of Lattimore's translation, published by them in 1962.

1963

33 (34) · ENCANTADAS

ENCANTADAS ‖ TWO SKETCHES ‖ FROM ‖ HERMAN
MELVILLE'S ‖ ENCHANTED ‖ ISLES ‖ WITH WOOD-
CUTS ‖ BY ‖ RICO LEBRUN ‖ PRINTED ‖ AT ‖ THE
GEHENNA PRESS ‖ IN ‖ NORTHAMPTON ‖ MCMLXIII

[line 1 in red]
With 6 woodcuts.
24 x 17½. 16 leaves & 6 [or 12] sheets, untrimmed. Printed in red & black.
CONTENTS: 2 blank leaves; (1) half title; (3) title page; (5) part title; (7) epigraph; (9-12) text; (13) part title; (15) epigraph; (17-19) text; (21) colophon, with pressmark XIV in red; 1 blank leaf; 6 [or 12] woodcuts, gathered within a single-folded untrimmed sheet of green Moriki; 2 blank leaves.
COLOPHON: "One hundred and fifty copies of this book have been printed at The Gehenna Press in Northampton, Massachusetts. The woodcuts were drawn on cherry blocks by Rico Lebrun and were cut by Leonard Baskin. The paper used for the text is Copperplate and Shogun for the Woodcuts. Harold McGrath was the pressman. Bembo is the type used throughout. The work finished during the month of March Mcmlxiii. *The edition is arranged as follows. Numbers 1-5 have a second suite of the woodcuts printed on Moriki a Japanese hand-made paper and are accompanied by an original drawing by Rico Lebrun. All the prints signed by the artist and the engraver. Numbers 6-31 have the second suite of woodcuts which along with impressions on Shogun are signed by the artist and the engraver. Numbers 32-150 have the single set of woodcuts and the colophon is signed by Rico Lebrun and Leonard Baskin. This is number* " Colophon numbered & signed by LB & Lebrun.
Not bound: copies 1-31 laid into a buckram-covered portfolio & enclosed in a leather & buckram slipcase, & copies 32-150 laid into a buckram-covered portfolio & enclosed in a buckram-covered slipcase, all by the Harcourt Bindery. A few copies were laid into a linen-covered portfolio & enclosed in a vellum & linen slipcase, by Gray Parrot, several years later.
4-page prospectus issued.

An ever growing fixture of the press [latterly abandoned] was to commission works from artists the printer admired. Thus evidenced in work by Shahn, Lockwood, Tyler, Cornell & others. The Encantadas, beyond the irradiated quality of Melville's prose, proved to be an apposite vehicle for the work of Rico

Lebrun. Lebrun was a match for Melville, his wonderful work was driven from that same boiling essence that Melville erupted from & Lebrun was propelled from the same furnace of unyielding probity; they were mighty. Lebrun responded to the first two sections of the Enchanted Isles, which is the entirety of Gehenna's 'Encantadas,' with a prodigious set of drawings on cherry-blocks of primordial tortoises which I happily cut, my knife paying faithful fealty to his drawn lines. The book's typography, the pages with their bestrewn masses of large sized Bembo, broadly meant to suggest a grand carapace, the vestment of the creatures that Lebrun humanizes. These venerables are variously displayed; one becomes Atlas, finding the world ever more hideously difficult to bear, & another shows his skeletonic cruciform, a mysterious but compelling revelation. Here also is the dragging ponderous immensity of the beasts & again they are grinding, hissing in mortal combat. A remarkable achievement to somehow extend Melville's meanings. Lebrun, although born in Naples, was very sensitive to nuances of English, he had masses of Dickinson & Auden by heart.

34 (32) · THE JOLLY BEGGARS

ROBERT BURNS ‖ THE JOLLY BEGGARS · *A CANTATA* ‖ EDITED BY JOHN C. WESTON ‖ THE GEHENNA PRESS ‖ NORTHAMPTON ‖ *MCMLXIII* [type within an arrangement of horizontal & vertical rules in red]
With a wood engraving by Gillian Lewis.
II x 9. 24 leaves, untrimmed. Printed in red & black.
CONTENTS: 2 blank leaves; (1) half title; (3) title page; (5) portrait of Burns; (7-18) text; (19) part title, "NOTES"; (21-28) editorial notes; (29-34) textual notes & variants; (35-37) afterword; (39) colophon, with pressmark VII in red; (41) pressmark XI; 1 blank leaf.
COLOPHON: "Three hundred copies of this book have been printed at the Gehenna Press in Northampton. Harold McGrath was the pressman. The text has been set in Monotype Bembo and is printed on Amalfi, a hand-made Italian paper. The wood-engraved portrait by Gillian Lewis has been printed from the block. The work finished during the month of June 1963 This is copy   " Colophon numbered.
Bound by Russell–Rutter Co. in French marbled paper over boards, with a Bancroft Linen spine & paper labels on the front cover & spine, & enclosed in a slipcase covered with the same paper.
4-page prospectus issued.
300 copies were also printed for the University of Massachusetts

Press. They are identical to the Gehenna Press edition except for the following: (1) the size of the book is 10¾ x 8½; (2) there are 5 leaves, rather than 3, before the title page [1 blank leaf; half title, followed by "PRINTED BY THE GEHENNA PRESS FOR THE UNIVERSITY OF MASSACHUSETTS PRESS"; 1 blank leaf; half title; 1 blank leaf], & thus the book has 26 leaves, not 24; (3) the colophon ends ". . . This is copy   Three hundred unnumbered copies have been printed on Warren's Oldstyle paper."; (4) the edition is bound in dark grey cloth over boards. This edition, though dated 1963, was not published until 1967.

35 (33) · ZODIAC

ZODIAC ‖ *The Twelve Signs* ‖ *Engraved on Wood* ‖ *by* ‖ *Sante Graziani* ‖ *with the* ‖ *Poems* ‖ *of* ‖ *Bertha Ten Eyck James* ‖ *1963* [first line in red]

11 x 8½. 20 leaves. Printed in italic on rectos only, in red & black. CONTENTS: 2 blank leaves; (1) half title; (3) title page; 1 blank leaf; (7-31) text & engravings; (33) colophon, with pressmark VII in red; (35) vignette.

COLOPHON: "Three hundred and fifty copies of this book have been printed at the Gehenna Press from the artists's [sic] wood blocks and Caslon type. Thirty copies have an extra suite of the wood engravings printed on Moriki the Japanese hand made paper. These impressions are signed by the artist. The thirty copies are quarter bound in leather with paper over boards. The balance of the edition is on Basingwerk paper quarterbound in cloth with paper over boards. This is copy number   " Colophon numbered. All copies enclosed in a slipcase, with an additional signed engraving on the front.

1-page prospectus issued.

1964

36 · THE DEFENSE OF GRACCHUS BABEUF

THE DEFENSE OF GRACCHUS BABEUF ‖ BEFORE THE HIGH COURT OF VENDOME ‖ [3½-inch rule] ‖ *EDITED &*

TRANSLATED ‖ WITH AN ESSAY ‖ ON BABEUF ‖ BY ‖ JOHN ANTHONY SCOTT ‖ [2½-inch rule in red] ‖ *WITH ‖ TWENTY-ONE ‖ ETCHED PORTRAITS ‖ BY ‖ THOMAS CORNELL ‖ THE GEHENNA PRESS ‖* NORTHAMPTON ‖ 1964 [first two lines in red]

12½ x 8¾. 48 leaves, untrimmed.

CONTENTS: 1 blank leaf; (i) half title; (ii) etched frontispiece; (iii) title page; 1-(60) text; 61-(64) *manifeste des égaux;* 65-(78) Francis-Noël Babeuf & the *conspiration des égaux;* 79-(84) biographical notes; 1 blank leaf; (87) colophon, with pressmark X in red; 1 blank leaf. The loose etchings, signed & with their titles printed blind, are interleaved throughout the book.

COLOPHON: "Three hundred copies of this book were printed at the Gehenna Press in Northampton, Mass., the work finished during March 1964. The type throughout is Baskerville. The paper is Nideggen made in Germany. Harold McGrath was the pressman. The suite of etchings were printed by Emiliano Sorini in New York. This is copy number   " Colophon signed & numbered by Cornell.

PAPER: etchings on blue Fabriano.

The unbound, unopened signatures are enclosed in a full leather chemise & laid into a leather & cloth traycase. Copies 1-50 contain a second suite of the etchings printed on large Rives [15 x 11], titled, numbered & signed by Cornell, in a cloth portfolio; these copies are in a larger traycase. Copies 1-21 also contain a drawing by Cornell. All work by Arno Werner.

12-page prospectus issued.

In some copies, the first suite of etchings is not interleaved, but follows the final blank.

In 1967 the University of Massachusetts Press issued a trade edition of the book.

It was in Edmund Wilson's "To the Finland Station" that I first read excerpts from Babeuf's long oration in self-defense [it took two weeks for him to deliver it.] Wanting to read it all, I repaired to the local library & then the inter-library benefice, but no English translation exists & the last French edition was

was issued in the mid-nineteenth century. Discussion with Sidney Kaplan ensued which resulted in the press' commissioning John Anthony Scott to translate & of necessity to severely edit the text, & the brilliant young artist Thomas Cornell devised a set of etchings of Babeuf & the principal players in his life & times. This book is an exemplar of an ideal that the press strove for in those years. A meaningful text, generally unavailable, set forth in handsome & apposite typography & enhanced with a set of etchings, woodcuts or lithographs, that enlarge or augment or deepen the text. To make this glorious work more widely known the University of Massachusetts Press published a popular edition of it.

37 · A LETTER FROM WILLIAM BLAKE

A LETTER FROM WILLIAM BLAKE ‖ [engraving] [type in red]

Letter from Blake to Thomas Butts, January 10, 1802. With 6 wood engravings by LB.

6 x 4½. 14 leaves, untrimmed. Printed in red & black.

CONTENTS: 1 blank leaf; (1) title page; (3-19) text & engravings; (21) colophon, with pressmark IV in red; (23) engraving; 1 blank leaf.

COLOPHON: "Five hundred copies of this letter have been printed at the Gehenna Press in Northampton. The woodengravings by Leonard Baskin have been printed from the blocks. Harold Mc-Grath was the pressman. Twenty-five copies have an additional suite of the woodengravings printed on Japanese vellum and are signed by the artist. They are hand-bound in full Oasis Niger Morocco. These copies are numbered I–XXV. Finished 30 May mcmlxiv. This is copy number   " Colophon numbered.

TYPE: Centaur; PAPER: Frankfurt, with 4 of the engravings on Moriki. The engravings are on pages (1), (5), (9), (15), (19) & (23). Three of the engravings are from *BLAKE AND THE YOUTHFUL ANCIENTS,* one is from that book's prospectus, & one is from *AUGURIES OF INNOCENCE.*

Copies 26–500 were sewn into boards, with wrappers of French marbled paper, & a paper label on the front cover.

1-page prospectus issued.

Some copies have one or two additional blanks, one initial & one final, & so have a total of 15 or 16 leaves.

Copies I–XXV have eight additional blanks, four initial & four final, & so have a total of 22 leaves. The additional suite of engravings is in a portfolio bound in after the first final blank.

38 · A HUMAN DOCUMENT

A HUMAN DOCUMENT ‖ ROBERT G. GARDNER ‖ THE GEHENNA PRESS ‖ 1964

With a wood engraving by LB.

9½ x 6. 10 leaves, untrimmed.

CONTENTS: 1 blank leaf; (1) title page; (3) note by Philip Hofer; (5-12) text; (13) colophon, with pressmark IV in red; (15) pressmark VI; 1 blank leaf. The engraving is printed at the head of the text on (5).

COLOPHON: "Five hundred copies were printed at The Gehenna Press in Northampton. The pressman was Harold McGrath. Centaur Monotype has been used throughout, and the paper is Frankfurt. The engraving by Leonard Baskin has been printed from the block. Work finished July, 1964. This is copy number　　　"

Colophon numbered.

Sewn into grey Fabriano wrappers, with A HUMAN DOCUMENT in black & a 2-inch rule in red printed on the front cover. 4-page prospectus issued.

25 copies contain an additional impression of the engraving, printed on Japanese vellum & signed by LB, laid in loosely.

39 · A BOOK OF MISCELLANEOUS BEASTS

A BOOK OF ‖ MISCELLANEOUS BEASTS ‖ FOR ‖ [name of recipient, handwritten by LB]

With 31 wood engravings, woodcuts & linoleum cuts by LB.

9½ x 9½. 33 leaves, untrimmed. Prnted on rectos only.

CONTENTS: (1) title page; (3-63) prints; (65) colophon, handwritten by LB.

COLOPHON: "5 copies printed at the Gehenna Press by Harold McGrath & Leonard Baskin 1964"

TYPE: American Uncial; PAPER: various Japanese papers.

Many of the blocks are reprinted from earlier Gehenna Press books.

Sewn into grey-green wrappers.

NVMMVS CONSORVM ROMANORVM [in red, with a coin printed from a line cut in grey below the type]
Keepsake No. 6. With 18 line cuts of Roman coins, printed in various colors.
4¾ x 5¼, oblong. 26 leaves, untrimmed, & diminishing in size towards the middle of the book, then increasing towards the end. Printed in red & black.
CONTENTS: 1 blank leaf; (1) title page; (3) dedication; (5-7) text from Addison's *Dialogues upon the Usefulness of Ancient Medals;* (9-41) coins; (43) colophon; (45) pressmark XII & date: "MCM-LXIV"; 2 blank leaves.
COLOPHON: "Keepsake number six Sixty copies of this keepsake were printed at the Gehenna Press in Northampton for the Friends and Patrons of the Press. Various European and Oriental papers were used. The cuts are taken from Huttichius/Imperatorum et Caesarum Vitae. Strassburg/W. Caephalaeus/1534. This is copy number   " Colophon numbered.
TYPE: American Uncial.
Sewn into blue-grey wrappers, with the coin from the title page printed blind on the front cover, & enclosed in a band of the same paper.

41 · REMBRANDT AND THE BOOK OF TOBIT

REMBRANDT AND THE BOOK OF TOBIT ‖ JULIUS HELD [fleuron in red] THE GEHENNA PRESS ‖ MCMLXIV
Gehenna Essays in Art, No. 2. With 50 reproductions of Rembrandt's paintings, drawings & etchings.
9¾ x 7¼. 48 leaves, untrimmed. Printed in red & black.
CONTENTS: 1 blank leaf; (1) series title; (3) title page; (5) dedication; (7)-(28) text; 29-(34) notes; (35) 4½-inch band of fleurons above a tipped-on errata slip, printed on Japanese paper; (37) part title, "THE PLATES"; (39-88) plates; 1 blank leaf; (91) colophon; 1 blank leaf.

COLOPHON: "1000 copies of this, the second volume of The Gehenna Essays in Art, have been printed at The Gehenna Press in Northampton, Massachusetts. The pressman was Harold McGrath. The plates have been printed at the Meriden Gravure Company, Meriden, Connecticut. The text has been set in Monotype Van Dijck and printed on paper specially made for this book by The Curtis Paper Company. Twenty-five copies have been bound at The Harcourt Bindery, Boston in one-half oasis niger, and are numbered 1 to 25. This is copy number   " Colophon numbered.

Copies 1–30 [not 1–25] bound in leather & grey paper over boards; the rest in green Fabriano over boards, with a Japanese vellum spine.

4-page prospectus issued.

1965
42 · CANCELLERESCA BASTARDA DISPLAYED

CANCELLERESCA BASTARDA ‖ DISPLAYED ‖ IN A SERIES ‖ OF MAXIMS AND MOTTOS ‖ WITH ALPHA-BETS AND ORNAMENTS ‖ THE GEHENNA PRESS ‖ MCMLXV [lines 1 & 7 in red]

6¼ x 5. 16 leaves, untrimmed. Printed in italic on rectos only in various colors.

CONTENTS: [foliated, not paginated] 1 blank leaf; (1) title page; 1–11 text; (12) translations; (13) colophon; (14) pressmark XVI in red.

COLOPHON: *"ONE HUNDRED COPIES PRINTED AT THE GEHENNA PRESS IN MARCH 1965 THIS IS COPY NUMBER   "* Colophon signed & numbered by LB.

PAPER: pre–World War II Amalfi, left unused by Bruce Rogers on his death.

Copies 1–10 bound by Arno Werner in full leather over boards.

Copies 11–100 bound in marbled paper, made by Peter Franck, over boards, with a paper label on the front cover.

Copies 1–10 have 38 leaves, not 16; their contents are as follows:

2 blank leaves; (i) title page; 1-11 text; (12) translations; (13) colophon; (14) pressmark XVI in red; 1 blank leaf; (16-26) text repeated; (27) translations repeated; 8 blank leaves. Leaves (16-27) are printed on Japanese vellum; leaves (16-26) are numbered 1-11.

Of all twentieth century type designers, I esteemed Jan van Krimpen & his beautiful faces the most. I reckoned that his Lutetia, Romanée, Cancelleresca Bastarda & Spectrum had no compeer for their compounding of strength with grace, their compaction of clarity with felicity & for their aspects of formal inevitability & their appearance of absolute perfection & immutability. The press had been slowly but steadily buying from J. Enschedé en Zonen fonts of van Krimpen's glorious calligraphic face Cancelleresca Bastarda & a little book displaying the type's three sizes, using mottos & apothegms, color & typographic ornaments was issued. It is modelled on type founders' & printers' custom to show the variety & diversity of a typeface in arranging inventive & typical examples of its possible & likely uses, & binding them up into a book.

43 · BETWEEN WARS AND OTHER POEMS
BETWEEN WARS ‖ AND OTHER POEMS ‖ [pressmark XVII in red] ‖ BY ANNE HALLEY ‖ *THE GEHENNA PRESS* ‖ *1965*
With 2 drawings by LB, printed from line cuts.
9 x 7. 36 leaves.
CONTENTS: 1 blank leaf; (3) half title; (5) title page; (7) dedication; (8-9) contents; (11) part title, "BETWEEN WARS"; 13-31 text; (32-33) drawings; (35) part title, "OTHER POEMS"; 37-69 text; (71) colophon, with pressmark XV.
COLOPHON: "Five hundred copies of this book have been printed by The Gehenna Press at Northampton, Massachusetts in Monotype Caslon on Cortlea. Harold McGrath was the pressman. The drawings are by Leonard Baskin; Some of the poems first appeared in *Intersection, The Massachusetts Review, Mutiny, The Noble Savage,* and *Perspective. . .* This is copy number   " Colophon numbered.
Bound in green cloth with a printed dust jacket.
1-page prospectus issued.
An edition of about 2000 copies was also printed for the University of Massachusetts Press. It is identical to the Gehenna Press edition except for the following: (1) *"THE GEHENNA PRESS"* on the title page is replaced by *"THE UNIVERSITY OF ‖ MASSACH-USETTS PRESS";* (2) page (6) has copyright information;

(3) pages 59-60 were reset; (4) there is an additional poem, *Mother Hubbard's Bones,* & consequently pages (8-9) & 66-70 were reset; (5) the colophon reads "Printed in Monotype Caslon on Strathmore Bouquet. The drawings are by Leonard Baskin; Some of the poems first appeared in *Intersection, The Massachusetts Review, Mutiny, The Noble Savage,* and *Perspective.",* is followed by a University of Massachusetts Press device, & is not numbered; (6) the edition is bound in stiff white paper.

An edition was also printed for the Oxford University Press. It is identical to the University of Massachusetts Press edition except for the following: (1) *"THE UNIVERSITY OF ‖ MASSACHUSETTS PRESS ‖ 1965"* on the title page is replaced by "THE UNIVERSITY OF ‖ MASSACHUSETTS PRESS ‖ LONDON: OXFORD UNIVERSITY PRESS ‖ *1966"*; (2) the colophon is followed by pressmark XV; (3) the edition is bound in red cloth with a printed dust jacket.

44 · CAPRICES & GROTESQUES

·CAPRICES & GROTESQUES· ‖ *DRAWINGS BY LEONARD BASKIN ‖ THE GEHENNA PRESS ‖ NORTHAMPTON ‖ MCMLXV* [line 1 in red, the title within a box of rules in black, the dots outside the box; date in red]

With 17 drawings by LB, printed from line cuts.

11 x 8. 20 leaves, untrimmed. Printed on rectos only, in red & black.

CONTENTS: 1 blank leaf; (1) title page; (3-33) drawings, five with captions; (35) colophon; 1 blank leaf.

COLOPHON: *"Five hundred copies printed at The Gehenna Press, Northampton, Massachusetts"*

TYPE: Cancelleresca Bastarda; PAPER: 5 tints of Fabriano, & 2 Japanese papers.

Sewn into grey Fabriano wrappers, & enclosed in a slipcase covered with the same paper, with a paper label on the front.

Ten copies contain an extra suite of the drawings on Japanese vellum, with the colophon signed by LB.

1-page prospectus issued.

45 · POEMS

POEMS ‖ MALCOLM W. BICK ‖ *Privately Printed* [first line in red]

8½ x 5½. 10 leaves, untrimmed.

CONTENTS: 1 blank leaf; (1) title page; (3) note by Michael Bick; (5-14) text; (15) colophon; 1 blank leaf.

COLOPHON: "25 copies printed at The Gehenna Press Northampton MCMLXV"

TYPE: Garamond; PAPER: Frankfurt.

Sewn into thin boards, with wrappers of marbled paper, made by Peter Franck, with a paper label on the front cover.

46 · A BOOK OF CREATURES

A BOOK OF CREATURES

With 70 wood engravings, woodcuts & linoleum cuts by LB, each one signed.

9 x 10, oblong. 74 leaves, untrimmed. Printed on rectos only.

CONTENTS: 1 blank leaf; (1) title page; (3-137) prints; 1 blank leaf; (141) print; (143) colophon, with wood engraved self-portrait, "LB ÆT 30"; 1 blank leaf.

COLOPHON: *"Printed at the Gehenna Press Northampton Mass. from blocks engraved by Leonard Baskin MCMLXV"*

TYPE: Cancelleresca Bastarda; PAPER: various Japanese papers.

Many of the blocks are reprinted from earlier Gehenna Press books.

Only a few copies were printed.

The book forms a single unsewn signature, which is laid into a portfolio of brown paper over boards, & enclosed in a slipcase covered with the same paper, with a paper label on the side.

1966

47 · GROSSMUTTI

GROSSMUTTI ‖ *A memoir compiled by her grandson Alex Page . . .* [12 lines, forming an inverted triangle] ‖ *Privately Printed* ‖ 1966

8¾ x 5¾. 6 leaves, untrimmed.

CONTENTS: I blank leaf; (1) title page; (3-8) text; (9) colophon, with pressmark VI.

COLOPHON: *"One hundred & fifty copies printed for Alex Page by his friends at The Gehenna Press in Northampton, Massachusetts. This is number* *"* Colophon numbered.

TYPE: Palatino; PAPER: a domestic machine-made paper.

Sewn into grey wrappers, with GROSSMUTTI in a box of rules printed on the front cover.

48 · THOMAS BIRD MOSHER

A CHECK LIST OF THE PUBLICATIONS OF ‖ THOMAS BIRD MOSHER OF PORTLAND ‖ MAINE ★ MDCCCXCI MDCCCCXXII ★ COM ‖ PILED & EDITED BY BENTON L. HATCH ‖ AND WITH A BIOGRAPHICAL ESSAY BY ‖ RAY NASH ★ PRINTED AT THE GEHENNA ‖ PRESS FOR THE UNIVERSITY OF ‖ MASSACHUSETTS PRESS ‖ [pressmark XVIII in red] ‖ MCMLXVI [first 3 words of line 2 & all asterisks in red]

With 3 illustrations & 19 facsimiles, all tipped-on.

10¾ x 7½. 108 leaves, untrimmed.

CONTENTS: I blank leaf; (3) half title; (5) title page; (7) contents; (8)-(32) biographical essay; 33-(39) preface & acknowledgements; 40-(43) list & description of the Mosher series; (45) part title, "A CHECK LIST OF THE ‖ PUBLICATIONS OF THOMAS BIRD MOSHER"; 47-(168) text; 169-(170) list of illustrations & facsimiles; 171-(212) index; (213) addenda, with pressmark XVI above text; (215) colophon, with pressmark XII in red.

COLOPHON: "500 copies of this book were printed at The Gehenna Press in Northampton for The University of Massachusetts Press in Amherst. The type is Monotype Van Dijck, the paper Fabriano. The facsimiles were printed from line engravings on Arches and on Shizuoka Vellum to simulate the papers used by Mosher. The three illustrations were reproduced by The Meriden Gravure Company in Meriden, Connecticut. The pressman was Harold

McGrath. Fifty copies, not for sale, are numbered I to L. This is copy number   " Copyright information follows. Colophon numbered.

The illustrations are on pages (8), (19) & (30), the facsimiles on (46), (50), (52), (56), (59), (61), (73), (77), (84), (89), (93), (103), (109), (116), (128), (130), (137), (144) & (163).

Bound by Russell–Rutter Co. in Bancroft Lynene & blue Fabriano over boards, with a paper label on the spine, & enclosed in a slip-case covered with the same paper, with the same paper label on the spine.

4-page prospectus issued.

An extra label is laid in between (216) & the endpaper. Presentation copies are accompanied by a slip, printed at The Gehenna Press, which reads "   is presented this copy no.   of *A Check List of the Publications of THOMAS BIRD MOSHER of Portland, Maine* as a token of my appreciation for your past assistance with the work. *Benton L. Hatch* ".

The ever rising costs of production, the idleness of McGrath & our inveterate incapacity to sell a sustaining capacity of books, impelled the press to offer its skills for occasional sale. We came then to design & print several books on demand. May I forthrightly confess that our losses in this enterprise were commensurate with normal practice. The intersticed densities of the prodigious Portland pirate, Thomas Bird Mosher, here all set forth in bibliographical order, caused a call on my subtlest typographical skills. The immense, dense & complex index is reflective of Mosher's endless manipulation of the same texts, set & issued in various sizes in divers series; it resolved itself into forty one pages set in eight point type. This is not the place to discuss or assess Mosher, but he was influential & important on many levels. The book was needed & its bibliographical avowals & endless index illuminate the tangled growth of his publishing tendencies.

49 · CONRAD'S MANIFESTO: PREFACE TO A CAREER

CONRAD'S MANIFESTO ‖ PREFACE TO A CAREER ‖ THE HISTORY OF THE ‖ PREFACE TO *THE NIGGER OF THE* ‖ *"NARCISSUS"* WITH FACSIMILES OF ‖ THE MANUSCRIPTS EDITED WITH ‖ AN ESSAY BY DAVID R. SMITH ‖ PHILADELPHIA ‖ MCMLXVI [lines 1, 2, 8 & 9 in red]

With a woodcut by LB.

11½ x 9. 42 leaves, untrimmed [facsimile leaves are trimmed.]
CONTENTS: (1) half title; (2) woodcut; (3) title page; (5) acknowledgements; (7) table of contents; 9-(14) foreword by Smith;
(15) part title, "THE MANUSCRIPTS: ‖ THE PREFACE TO
THE N OF THE "N" ‖ TO MY READERS IN AMERICA";
(16) note on facsimiles; (17-32) facsimiles; (33) part title, "TRAN-
SCRIPTIONS OF THE MANUSCRIPTS"; (34) note on tran-
scriptions; 35-(42) transcriptions; 43-(46) preface, as published in
1902; 47-(77) essay by Smith; 78-(79) footnotes; (81) colophon,
with pressmark XVI in red above text & pressmark VI in red below
text; 1 blank leaf.
COLOPHON: "1100 COPIES OF THIS BOOK PRINTED AT
THE GEHENNA PRESS NORTHAMPTON, MASSACH-
USETTS FOR THE PHILIP H. AND A.S.W. ROSENBACH
FOUNDATION PHILADELPHIA, PENNSYLVANIA. THE
FACSIMILES WERE MADE BY THE MERIDEN GRAVURE
COMPANY OF MERIDEN, CONNECTICUT. THE TEXT
IS SET IN MONOTYPE VAN DIJCK. THE PAPER IS
FABRIANO. HAROLD MCGRATH WAS THE PRESSMAN.
THE WOODCUT PORTRAIT OF JOSEPH CONRAD BY
LEONARD BASKIN WAS PRINTED FROM THE BLOCK.
COPIES I TO C HAVE AN ADDITIONAL IMPRESSION OF
THE PORTRAIT PRINTED ON SHIZUOKA VELLUM
AND ARE SIGNED BY THE ARTIST. COPYRIGHT © 1966.
THE WORK FINISHED DURING THE FALL OF 1966. THIS
IS COPY NUMBER   " Colophon numbered.
Bound by Russell-Rutter Co. in French marbled paper over boards,
with a paper label on the front cover, & enclosed in a chemise of
grey paper over boards & a slipcase covered with the same paper,
with a paper label on the spine.
4-page prospectus issued.
A few hundred copies were acquired from the Rosenbach Foundation by David R. Godine, Publisher, of Boston in 1974. 250
copies were sold to The Bodley Head, London, by Godine; they

were issued with a Bodley Head label on the spine of the slipcase. The rest were issued with a Godine label on the spine of the slipcase. Both labels were printed at The Godine Press.

1967

50 · AN EVENING'S JOURNEY TO CONWAY MASSACHUSETTS

ARCHIBALD MACLEISH ‖ [3¼-inch rule in red] ‖ AN EVENING'S JOURNEY TO ‖ CONWAY MASSACHUSETTS ‖ *AN OUTDOOR PLAY* ‖ WRITTEN FOR THE BICENTENNIAL OF THE TOWN OF CONWAY ‖ 1767-1967 [date in red]
With a wood engraving by LB.
10 x 7. 14 leaves, untrimmed.
CONTENTS: (i) blank; (ii) "visionary portrait" of MacLeish; (1) title page; (2) copyright; (3) dedication & note; (5)-(21) text; (23) colophon; (25) pressmark XIX.
COLOPHON: *"PRINTED AT THE GEHENNA PRESS, NORTHAMPTON, MASSACHUSETTS, 1967."*
TYPE: Centaur & Arrighi; PAPER: Nideggen.
400 copies printed.
Sewn into blue Fabriano wrappers, & enclosed in a slipcase covered with the same paper, with a paper label on the front.
In some copies, pages (2) & (23) are blank.
Twenty-five copies, numbered I–XXV, have an additional impression of the wood engraving signed by the artist & are bound in paper over boards.
An edition on Mohawk Suede Finish, lacking the engraving & pressmark, was also printed; this edition was sewn into green wrappers, with the title printed on the front cover.

51 · FLOSCULI SENTENTIARUM

FLOSCULI ‖ SENTENTIARUM ‖ [1⅝-inch band of fleurons in yellow] ‖ PRINTERS·FLOWERS ‖ MORALISED [lines 1 & 2 in red; lines 3 & 4 in green; all within an oval border]
A series of aphorisms, joined to arrangements of fleurons formerly

belonging to Bruce Rogers; with an essay by Dale Roylance. 11½ x 8. 32 leaves, untrimmed. Printed on rectos only in various colors.

CONTENTS: [foliated, not paginated] 1 blank leaf; (1) title page; 2-(27) text; 28-(29) essay; (30) translations; (31) colophon, with pressmark VII in red.

COLOPHON: "Two hundred and fifty copies of Flosculi Sententiarum were printed at the Gehenna Press in Northampton, Massachusetts. The work finished during March, 1967. The ornaments were arranged by Leonard Baskin. Harold McGrath was the pressman. The typeface used throughout is Centaur designed by Bruce Rogers. The paper was hand made in France in 1905 for Warren H. Colson of Boston, and acquired by the press from an antiquarian bookseller in 1959. Fifty copies have been specially bound by Arno Werner of Pittsfield, Massachusetts and carry the Roman numerals I through L. This is copy number" Numbered within a box of four fleurons.

Bound by Arno Werner. Copies I-L bound in full leather, and laid into a leather & cloth traycase; copies 51-250 bound in vellum & marbled paper over boards.

Most copies have an additional 1 or 3 initial blanks, & an additional 1 or 3 final blanks.

4-page prospectus issued.

The Arts of the Book division of Yale's Sterling Memorial Library held a collection of ornaments, devices, culs de lamps, etc. that had belonged to Bruce Rogers; they were venerated if entirely unused. The keeper of these reliques, these printers' flowers & decorative elements had the bright notion of making a display book from the photo-mechanical & leaden ornaments. I had ever been interested in those marvellous flowers, that grow in the hidden garden of printers' cases, & their usage, both scant & profuse, by earlier printers. I was delighted when asked to arrange & order the Yale Rogers' fleurons, rosselins, vignettes, & to tie apothegms & mottos to them & render them sentient. The book is a 'tour de force' of typographic play; one page passed through the press nine times to achieve its diversity of color & gold. Dale Roylance, then curator of Yale's Book Arts collection & now at Princeton, wrote a sparkling two pages on Gehenna, its endeavor, its qualities & its achievements. Flosculi glows, the color flashing off its pages & I think pressing an older formulation onward.

[drawing] ‖ HERMAN MELVILLE · *A THOUGHT ON BOOK-BINDING* [type in red]

With a drawing by LB, printed from a line cut.

12 x 9. 4 leaves, unopened. Printed in red & black.

CONTENTS: (1) title page; (4-5) text; (8) colophon, with pressmark XXb in red.

COLOPHON: *"Herman Melville wrote this review of Cooper's* The Red Rover *for* The Literary World *(VI, March 16, 1850, pp. 276-7) while he was at work on* Moby-Dick. *Typography by Leonard Baskin, who drew the portrait of Melville, aet. 31; editorial assistance by Sidney Kaplan; presswork by Harold McGrath. Monotype Van Dijck by Mackenzie & Harris, San Francisco; letterpress on Clear Spring Brook ["Brook" deleted with a red rule, & corrected to "Book" in red in the margin] Antique by West Virginia Pulp and Paper Company. Printed by The Gehenna Press, Northampton, Massachusetts, June, 1967."*

This text was originally to be printed as a keepsake; a few copies were printed in early 1964, but the full edition was not printed, & the project was temporarily abandoned. The following is a description of this "first printing."

A THOUGHT ON BOOKBINDING ‖ [engraving of Melville] [type in red]

With a wood engraving by LB.

7¾ x 5. 6 leaves, untrimmed.

CONTENTS: (1) title page; (2) dedication; (3-6) text; (7) textual note & note on the engraving; (9) colophon, with pressmark VI in red; 1 blank leaf.

COLOPHON: "One hundred copies of this keepsake were printed at The Gehenna Press in Northampton for the friends and patrons of the press. Finished the first week of 1964"

TYPE: Perpetua.

53 · AESOPIC

AESOPIC ‖ TWENTY FOUR COUPLETS BY ANTHONY HECHT TO ACCOMPANY ‖ THE THOMAS BEWICK

WOOD ENGRAVINGS FOR · SELECT FABLES · ‖ WITH
AN AFTERWORD ON THE BLOCKS BY PHILIP HOFER ‖
[5¼–inch rule in red] ‖ AT THE GEHENNA PRESS IN NOR-
THAMPTON · MASSACHUSETTS [first line in red]

7¾ x 8¼, oblong. 20 leaves, untrimmed. Printed in italic, in red &
black.

CONTENTS: 1 blank leaf; (1) title page; (3-26) text & engravings;
(27) part title, *"A note on Bewick's Blocks"*; (29) note; (31) colophon,
with pressmark XII in red; 3 blank leaves.

COLOPHON: *"Five hundred copies of Aesopic were printed at The Gehenna Press in Palatino type on Arches paper. Fifty copies, numbered I to L,
contain a suite of twenty-four woodengravings on Sekishu, a Japanese
paper and are specially bound. The pressman was Harold McGrath. The
word Aesopic on the title was lettered by John E. Benson. The Bewick
blocks were lent by Philip Hofer. One hundred copies have been set aside
for The Society of Printers, Boston. These copies bear the Society's mark
and contain an additional engraving. The work was finished during the
summer of 1967. This is copy number* *"*Colophon signed &
numbered by LB.

Bound by Robert Burlen of Boston in green Fabriano over boards,
with a paper label on the spine. The copies for The Society of
Printers are bound in brown Fabriano over boards, with the same
paper label on the spine. In copies I-L, the second suite of engravings is in a separate portfolio, & the book & the portfolio are
enclosed in a slipcase covered with blue–grey Fabriano, with a
paper label on the front.

*Philip Hofer was an extraordinarily prescient collector of books & drawings of mainly the sixteenth but
other centuries as well. His benefactions to Harvard were vast & the treasures he gave are housed at the
Houghton Library. Hofer, of mercurial temperament, was a friend of the press & one day he offered
the press the use of eighty-four blocks that Bewick had engraved for an edition of 'Select Fables'. The
moralizing intent of the engravings suggested another emblem book & Aesopic is the result. Again
Anthony Hecht, a poet much interested in poetic forms, was called upon & he endowed the book with
twenty-four brilliant epigrammatic couplets. Building make-readies for Bewick's lowered blocks was a
very special & interesting task & attaching two lines of felicitous type proved a book-making delight. A
small edition without text was printed of all the blocks.*

THE MATCHMAKER'S LAMENT ‖ AND OTHER ‖ ASTON-ISHMENTS ‖ POEMS BY LEONARD NATHAN ‖ [3⅛-inch rule in red] ‖ *DRAWINGS BY LEONARD BASKIN ‖ Again, if two lie together, then they ‖ have heat; but how can one be warm alone? Eccl. 4, 11 ‖ THE GEHENNA PRESS · NORTHAMPTON · 1967 ‖* [3⅛-inch rule in red] [lines 1-3 in red]

With marginal drawings throughout, reproduced by offset.

11 x 8. 16 leaves. Printed in italic, in red & black.

CONTENTS: 2 blank leaves; (1) half title; (3) title page; (5) contents; (7-24) text & drawings; (25) colophon, with pressmark XXI in red; 1 blank leaf.

COLOPHON: *''Four hundred copies of this book have been printed at the Gehenna Press in Northampton, Massachusetts. The typeface throughout is Arrighi; the paper Arches, made in France. The printing was completed in the fall of 1967. The pressman was Harold McGrath, the drawings were reproduced by the Meriden Gravure Company of Connecticut. An etching by Leonard Baskin and signed by him accompanies copies numbered I-L. This is copy number.   ''*Colophon numbered.

Bound in brown paper over boards, with a paper label on the spine. The etching is laid in loosely.

A number of copies suffered damage to their spines in storage.

I was moved by Nathan's trenchantly ironic poems and was pleased to have the chance to make drawings to them. I rather think the book is too heavily freighted with drawings. The beautiful, light Arrighi types seem battered, assaulted, overwhelmed by them. The paper was poorly chosen, it too seems too heavily charged, too laden, incapable of carrying this burden of illustration. A great lesson was learned from this overloading, the urgent necessity of spatial relationship was borne upon me & the interaction of space & weight, the sizes of type, the density of paper, the number & range of illustrations, & how they work one upon the other.

1968

55 (56) · SELECT FABLES

Bewicks · Select Fables · Impressions from 84 blocks ‖ The Gehenna Press [text of line 1 in red, dots in black]

Blocks used in the 1776 & 1784 editions of *Select Fables,* lent to the press by Philip Hofer.

7 x 5. 90 leaves, untrimmed. Printed in italic on rectos only, in red & black.

CONTENTS: 1 blank leaf; (1) title page; (3) note; (5-171) engravings; (173) colophon; (175) pressmark XIX in red; 1 blank leaf.

COLOPHON: *"Thirty five copies printed in Northampton · 1968"*

TYPE: Palatino; PAPER: Nideggen & Sekishu.

Bound by Arno Werner in full vellum & laid into a vellum & cloth traycase.

Much of the edition was destroyed by water damage at the press in 1970. The 14 copies that survived were not bound until later that year.

56 (55) · CULS DE LAMPE

CULS ‖ DE ‖ LAMPE ‖ [3 dots in red] ‖ The ‖ Gehenna ‖ Press [type within a line cut of a woodcut from a 17th century book] Woodcut headpieces & tailpieces from 16th & 17th century books, printed from line cuts in various colors.

6 x 6½, oblong. 28 leaves, untrimmed. Printed on rectos only in red & black.

CONTENTS: [foliated, not paginated] 1 blank leaf; (1) title page; 2-20 culs de lampe; (21) list of sources; (22) colophon; (23) pressmark XXIII in red; 4 blank leaves.

COLOPHON: "250 copies of Culs de Lampe have been printed at The Gehenna Press, Northampton, Massachusetts. The papers are Nideggen and Fabriano blue and white. Harold McGrath was the pressman. The work finished April 1968."

TYPE: Centaur.

About 80 copies were bound by Arno Werner in marbled paper over boards, with an imitation vellum spine. The rest were later bound by Gray Parrot in marbled paper over boards, with a label on the spine; these copies contain an additional 4 blank leaves, 3 before the title page & one immediately following it. A few of the copies bound by Parrot were laid into a leather & cloth traycase.

SCHOLASTIC DIALOGUE [in blue]

10 x 6½. 12 leaves, untrimmed. Printed in various colors.
CONTENTS: 3 blank leaves; (1) the letters "G P" surrounded by an arrangement of fleurons; (3) title page; (5) dedication; (7–11) text; (13) colophon; 2 blank leaves.

COLOPHON: "Printed in an edition of 25 copies at The Gehenna Press Northampton, Massachusetts June 1968 The method of teaching by means of question and answer was prevalent in the medieval cathedral schools; this form of catechism was an outgrowth of the Socratic Method handed down through the writings of Plato.···· This dialogue is from *Disputatio Regalis et Nobilissimi Iuvenis Pippini cum Albino Scholastico* Alcuin: 8th century. Alcuin (Albinus) was the the tutor of Pippin, son of Charlemagne."

TYPE: Binney Oldstyle; PAPER: Amalfi.

Bound by Arno Werner. Sewn into marbled paper over stiff paper wrappers. Some copies were bound in full leather & laid into a leather & cloth traycase; these copies have an additional 40 final blanks.

This wondrous catechistic dialogue nudges at reality with medieval dialectics informed by Socratic methods of probing, questioning, followed by the most pithy of responses. This short marvel was printed for a friend of the press, Edwin Rome, who profoundly fancied it. Rome was a very distinguished Philadelphia lawyer & a collector of choice English watercolors & illustrated books. Was it the quality of the incisive & acuminous cross-examination that attracted Rome? I presume so & and am thankful for it.

[engraving] ‖ THERE WAS A CHILD WENT FORTH ‖ WALT WHITMAN ‖ *WOOD ENGRAVINGS BY GILLIAN TYLER* [line 2 in red]

With 10 wood engravings.

12 x 10¾. 14 leaves. Printed on rectos only in red & black.
CONTENTS: 1 blank leaf; (1) half title; (3) title page; (5–19) text & engravings; (21) engraving; (23) colophon, with Tyler pressmark; 1 blank leaf.

COLOPHON: "Two hundred copies of this book were printed at
The Gehenna Press at Northampton in 1968. The wood engrav-
ings were printed from the blocks. Harold McGrath was the
pressman. One hundred copies, numbered 1–100 are on Nideggen.
One hundred unnumbered copies are on Mead's Suede Book."
Copies 1–100 signed & numbered by Tyler.
TYPE: Perpetua.
Bound in marbled paper over boards, with an imitation vellum
spine, & enclosed in a slipcase covered with the same paper.

59 · WOODCUT
WANG ‖ HUI- ‖ MING ‖ *WOOD* ‖ *CUT-* ‖ *EPOH* ‖ *STUDIO*
[text printed from a woodcut]
With 9 woodcuts, each signed & numbered by Wang. The book
reads "from back to front" in the manner of books printed in
languages that read from right to left.
9½ x 6½. 30 leaves, untrimmed. Printed on rectos only in various
colors.
CONTENTS: (1) Chinese calligraphic title, printed from a woodcut;
(3) dedication; 1 blank leaf; (7) title page; (9) 3 poems by Robert Bly;
1 blank leaf; (13) blank; (14) Chinese calligraphy, printed from a
woodcut; (15) poem by Po Chü-I; 2 blank leaves; (21–53) woodcuts;
1 blank leaf; (57) colophon, with Wang pressmark in red; 1 blank leaf.
COLOPHON: "This portfolio was issued in a limited edition of one
hundred copies of signed and numbered original prints, designed
and printed at the Epoh Studio, Amherst, Massachusetts by
Wang Hui-Ming in October, 1968. The English text was hand
set Palatino Roman and printed on Nideggen paper by Harold
McGrath at The Gehenna Press in Northampton, Massachusetts.
The slipcase was specially made by Arno Werner of Pittsfield,
Massachusetts and the paper used for the prints was Rives. This is
copy number __" Colophon numbered.
Not bound; enclosed in a stiff wrapper & laid into a cloth traycase.
4-page prospectus issued.

[engraving] ‖ ·.· SAMUEL SEWALL ·.· ‖ ·.· ‖ THE SELLING OF JOSEPH ‖ A MEMORIAL ‖ *THE GEHENNA PRESS* ‖ *MCMLXVIII* [lines 2 & 3 in red]

The Gehenna Tracts, No. 1. With a wood engraving by LB & an essay by Sidney Kaplan.

8 ¼ x 5 ¾. 38 leaves, untrimmed. Printed in red & black.

CONTENTS: 2 blank leaves; (1) series title; (3) title page; (5)-15 text; 17-(24) notes; (25)-(51) essay by Kaplan; (52)-(61) notes; (62)-(65) bibliography; (67) colophon, with pressmark XVIII in red; 2 blank leaves.

COLOPHON: *"One hundred copies were printed at The Gehenna Press during the winter of 1968-9. The portrait of Sewall, printed from the block, was engraved by Leonard Baskin. Each copy is accompanied by an additional impression of the portrait, signed by the artist, on Japanese paper. The pressman was Harold McGrath. The editor was Sidney Kaplan . . . This is copy* "Colophon numbered.

TYPE: Binney Oldstyle; PAPER: a French paper, hand made in 1905 for Warren H. Colson of Boston.

Bound by Arno Werner in leather & marbled paper over boards. The impression of the portrait on Japanese paper is laid in loosely. Some copies were destroyed by water damage at the press in 1970. In 1969 the University of Massachusetts Press issued a trade edition of about 3000 copies, printed from the same type, but not at The Gehenna Press.

The Gehenna Tracts, instituted with 'The Selling of Joseph', is expressive of Sidney Kaplan's editorial role in providing to the press generally inaccessible texts of importance. The series of tracts represented an attempt to make available works that touch in a crucial way a moment in the history of the struggle for freedom & a more just ordering within society. It may be said that these meaningful texts typified an aspect of the press' interests & concerns in those years & bespeak Kaplan's generative presence. A popular edition was published by the University of Massachusetts Press.

1969

61 · BRESDIN TO REDON

BRESDIN TO REDON ‖ *six letters 1870 to 1881* ‖ *edited by Roseline*

Bacou ‖ translated by Seymour S Weiner ‖ The Gehenna Press ‖ 1969
[lines 1 & 5 in red]
With an etching by LB.
10 x 6. 30 leaves, untrimmed. Printed in red & black.
CONTENTS: 1 blank leaf; (1) half title; (3) title page; (5) etching; (7-9) note on Bresdin; (10) note on the letters; (11-18) text; (19-21) notes; (23) colophon, with pressmark XVIII in red; 17 blank leaves.
COLOPHON: "Four hundred copies have been printed on a Japanese paper in monotype Centaur and Arrighi. A double portrait of Bresdin and Redon, etched by Leonard Baskin, is printed from the plate. The first hundred copies, specially bound, have an additional impression of the etching signed by the artist. The pressman was Harold P. McGrath. The text is a chapter from *Lettres de gauguin, gide, huysmans, jammes, mallarmé, verhaeren . . . à Odilon Redon, présentées par Arï Redon . . . textes et notes par Roseline Bacou*, published by Librairie José Corti, Paris, 1960 . . . This is copy number   "
Colophon signed & numbered by LB.
PAPER: Japanese Etching.
Copies 1-100 bound by Arno Werner in full leather & laid into a leather & marbled paper traycase. The additional impression of the etching is laid in loosely. Some of these copies suffered water damage at the press in 1970. Copies 101-400 bound by Gray Parrot in leather & marbled paper over boards; these copies have two additional blanks, one initial & one final, & so have a total of 32 leaves. Copies 101-400 were bound gradually; work began in 1975, and at the time of writing most of the edition had been bound.

Rodolphe Bresdin, the Maître au Lapin, the hero of Champfleury's "Chien Caillu", the ardent dreamer of virgin forests, the deviser of the densest & most tangled woods, a breathtaking fantasist of haunted chateaux & of skeletons animating the spidered deep of his enchanted forests, was of intense interest to the printer, who had managed to collect fifty-five drawings & forty-five prints by this elusive & bemused master, whose renown rested in his being the teacher of Redon, who signed his first six prints, "élève de Bresdin." This wondrous & mysterious etcher & lithographer was the subject of a promised but still undelivered Gehenna Essay in Art. These letters, taken from a popularly published larger context of artists' letters, was an opportunity to put Bresdin's name before an American audience. This little book dangerously wants a larger substance but the press takes some mitigation in having caused the translating & printing of six of Bresdin's letters.

EVRIPIDES · HIPPOLYTOS · TRANSLATED BY ‖ ROBERT
BAGG · ILLUSTRATED BY ‖ LEONARD BASKIN · PRIN-
TED AT ‖ THE GEHENNA PRESS · NORTHAMPTON ‖
MCMLXIX [second word of line 1 in red]

With 10 etchings.

19 x 12½. 40 leaves, untrimmed. Printed in red & black.

CONTENTS: 1 blank leaf; (1) half title; (3) title page; (5) dramatis personae; (7–72) text; 1 blank leaf; (75) colophon, with pressmark XIV
in red; 1 blank leaf.

COLOPHON: "Two hundred copies of Euripides' *Hippolytos* were
printed at The Gehenna Press in Northampton, Massachusetts,
the work completed during the summer of 1969. The type is
Monotype Centaur and Arrighi. The pressman was Harold
McGrath. The etchings by Leonard Baskin were printed from
the plates by Emiliano Sorini. The translator thanks John Moore
of Amherst College for his help with the Greek text; George
Dimock of Smith College, William Arrowsmith, James Hynd and
Thomas Gould of the University of Texas for their comments on
the manuscript; and Atheneum Publishers for permission to use
the text in its present form. W. S. Barrett's edition of the play,
published by Oxford University Press, was followed throughout.
The translation is dedicated to Theodore Ely Bagg and Elma
White Bagg. . . This is copy number   " Colophon signed &
numbered by LB.

Copies 1–100 were for sale.

Bound by Arno Werner in leather & marbled paper over boards,
with the etchings in a portfolio of cloth & marbled paper over
boards, the whole laid into a leather & marbled paper traycase.

Some copies have an additional 2 initial blanks; some have an additional 2 or 4 final blanks.

4-page prospectus issued.

I had until recently considered the 'Hippolytos' as being Gehenna's finest typographic achievement.
There is an enriched seemliness, a measured justness, an enhanced rightness in the printed text, all

building towards a quality of arranged inevitability. These felicities rest on strong structures of organiza-tion, the size of type & its relatedness to the size & weight of the paper, how the head & outer margins pertain & resonate with the gutter & how these nuances of subjectively judged or felt elements create the higher harmonies that typography adduces. The strong & beautiful Centaur types are printed, indeed, stamped into the fabric of the paper with so correctly assessed quantities of ink, that the intensity & perfected beauty of the type is clearly & glowingly revealed. The type & paper merge, become as one in ineluctable & desirable fusion, pleasurable to our eyes & enhansive to the text. The superb translation by Robert Bagg was undertaken at the behest of the press. The etchings I made, I now clearly see, were in-different & irrelevant, unilluminative & uninstructive & altogether of a poor insufficiency when thought of in conjunction with Euripides' profound & tragic Phaedra & the other perplexed humans in whose lives the gods of Olympus so wantonly played. I must have had a sense of the prints' inadequacy for I had them housed in a separate porfolio, tucked into a box behind the bound signatures of the play. I have since worked with the theme of Phaedra & feel that I am now up to the task of illustrating it. I am thankful that the typographic unity & beauty of the Gehenna Hippolytos is unsullied.

63 · LAUS PICTORUM

LAVS PICTORVM ‖ PORTRAITS OF NINETEENTH ‖ CENTURY ARTISTS INVENTED ‖ AND ENGRAVED BY LEONARD ‖ BASKIN THE GEHENNA PRESS ‖ NORTH-AMPTON [first line in red]

With 10 wood engravings & 5 etchings, one printed in green & black.

14 x 11. 6 leaves, excluding the prints & mats. Printed in red & black.

CONTENTS: 1 blank leaf; (1) title page; prints, matted, with their titles printed blind on the mats; (3) part title, "NOTES ON THE ARTISTS"; (4-8) notes; (9) colophon, with pressmark XX in black & red.

COLOPHON: "The edition of *LAVS PICTORVM* is arranged as follows: one hundred copies have a double set of the portraits, both sets matted, numbered I to C: seventy-five copies have in addition to a matted set an extra suite of the portraits and are numbered CI to CLXXV: one hundred & seventy-five copies have a single set of matted portraits and are numbered 1 to 175. A group of artist's sets are lettered A to ZZ. All the prints are signed. Harold McGrath was the pressman. The paper has been specially made by the Strathmore Paper Company & is pure. The chemises & cases have been made by Arno Werner of Pittsfield, Mass. The

work finished, fall 1969. This is copy number   " Colophon
signed & numbered by LB.

TYPE: Centaur.

The engravings of Morris & Eakins are reprinted from a broadside
& a keepsake, respectively.

Not bound; enclosed in a full leather chemise & laid into a leather
& marbled paper traycase, by Arno Werner.

16-page prospectus, not printed at The Gehenna Press, issued by
the publisher, A. Lublin, Inc., New York.

In 1971 CFA Graphics, New York, liquidated what remained of the
edition; many copies were consequently broken, & the prints sold
individually.

*Laus Pictorum was the second in a series of collected portraits which the press issued. This excessive love
of iconologias [seven have thus far been published] last found expression in "Icones Librorum Artifices",
& at this moment of writing, in the unfinished "Semblant," "Death Masks" & "Jewish Artists of the
Early & Late Renaissance". Portrait engravings have long been a special interest of the printer, who has
gathered a large number of earlier examples. It was an illusion of the printer who thought that his making of a near endless number of portraits of earlier artists was done in purest homage, discovered on deeper
consideration that they functioned as much as a reaching-out for succor & assistance, as anything else.
The justification of the edition, as expressed in the colophon, was influenced by the editions truffé of
French Livres de Peintres & does not, I fear, make much sense.*

64 · THE BIRDS AND THE ANIMALS

[3 woodcut Chinese calligraphic characters, in green] ‖ THE
BIRDS AND THE ANIMALS ‖ WANG HUI-MING ‖ THE
GEHENNA PRESS

With 21 woodcuts, printed in various colors.

10 x 7. 25 sheets, untrimmed. Printed on rectos only in red & black.

CONTENTS: (1) title page; (2) Chinese calligraphy, printed from
a woodcut, & translation; (3) dedication; (4-24) woodcuts;
(25) colophon.

COLOPHON: *"Two hundred copies of The Birds and the Animals by the
reincarnated Sung Master Wang Hui-Ming were printed from his original
blocks at Northampton Massachusetts during October 1969. All copies
have each print signed by the Artist. Nine oriental papers were used. The*

pressman was Harold McGrath. This is copy number   '' Colophon
numbered.
TYPE: Centaur & Arrighi.
Not bound; enclosed in a stiff wrapper & laid into a leather & cloth
traycase, by Arno Werner.

1970
65 (128) · CABLE TO GARDINER
CABLE TO GARDINER ‖ [line cut of a flower, in green]
Facsimile of a letter from George Cable to Harry Norman
Gardiner, July 13, 1901, with a note by Daniel Aaron.
9 x 5¾. 8 leaves.
CONTENTS: 2 blank leaves; (1) title page; (3) letter; (5-7) note;
(9) colophon, with pressmark XXIV in green & red; 1 blank leaf.
COLOPHON: *''2000 copies printed at the Gehenna Press in Northampton
as a keepsake for the Friends of the Smith College Library''*
Stapled into grey–brown wrappers, with CABLE TO GAR-
DINER in a box of rules printed on the front cover.

66 (65) · WEST–ÖSTLICHER DIVAN
WEST-ÖSTLICHER DIVAN ‖ GOETHE'S WEST-
EASTERN DIVAN ‖ TRANSLATION & COMMENTARY
BY ‖ ALEX PAGE ‖ DRAWINGS BY ‖ LEONARD BASKIN ‖
VOLUME ONE ‖ THE FIRST SEVEN BOOKS ‖ THE
GEHENNA PRESS · MCMLXX [lines 1 & 7 in red]
Bilingual edition. With marginal drawings throughout, printed
from line cuts.
7¾ x 4¼. 128 leaves. Printed in red & black.
CONTENTS: 1 blank leaf; (i) half title; (ii) frontispiece; (1) title page;
(3) contents; 4-231 text & drawings; 233-236 notes; 237-(244) after-
word; (245) colophon, with pressmark XXV in red; 3 blank leaves.
COLOPHON: *''Three hundred copies were printed at The Gehenna Press
in Northampton, Massachusetts during the summer of 1970. The type is
Baskerville monotype, the paper Monadnock WvG. The drawings were
made by Leonard Baskin. Copies 1-100 carry an additional etched portrait*

*of Goethe, signed by the artist, on Japanese paper. The pressman was
Harold McGrath . . . This is copy   "* Colophon numbered.
Bound by John Newman of Dublin in red cloth over boards &
enclosed in a slipcase covered with marbled paper.
The last two signatures were inadvertently reversed. The final four
leaves are bound between 236 & 237.
LB made two etched portraits of Goethe, but very few copies of
the book were issued with either one.
Although it was printed in 1970, & bound in 1973, the book was not
published until 1975.
About a dozen copies were recased in leather & marbled paper
over boards by Gray Parrot in 1988.

*The syndics of the press were astounded to discover that no twentieth-century translation existed of
Goethe's "West-Östlicher Divan," his old-age erotic fantasies in Sufiesque poetic fashion. Calling
upon the great skill of Alex Page, virtually the Press' resident translator from the German, the first
volume of an intended three volume edition was printed. The translation is incisive & compelling &
Page's invention was assisted by the paralleled presence of the German. My drawings often tend to leap
across the double pages, perhaps hoping somehow to bridge the German & the English.*

67 (66) · ALCUIN

ALCUIN: ‖ A DIALOGUE ‖ CHARLES BROCKDEN
BROWN ‖ EDITED WITH AN AFTERWORD ‖ BY LEE R.
EDWARDS ‖ [drawing] ‖ THE GEHENNA PRESS MCMLXX
[first word of line 1 in green; line 3 in red]
The Gehenna Tracts, No. 3. With a drawing by LB, printed from
a line cut.
$8\frac{1}{4}$ x $5\frac{3}{4}$. 56 leaves. Printed in red & black.
CONTENTS: [paginated unconventionally: even pages are rectos,
odd pages versos] 1 blank leaf; (ii) series title; (2) title page; (4)-88 text;
89-90 notes; 92-(104) afterword; (106) colophon, with pressmark
VI in green; 1 blank leaf.
COLOPHON: *"Three hundred copies were printed at The Gehenna Press,
Northampton, Massachusetts during the summer of 1970. The type is
Centaur & Arrighi, the paper Monadnock WvG. The portrait is by
Leonard Baskin. Copies 1-100 carry an additional etched portrait of*

Brown, signed by the artist, on Japanese paper. The pressman was Harold McGrath . . . This is copy   " Colophon signed & numbered by LB. Bound by John Newman of Dublin in red cloth over boards & enclosed in a slipcase covered with marbled paper. The etching is laid in loosely.

Copies 1-100 were actually numbered I-C; the rest of the edition was numbered 1-200.

Although it was printed in 1970, & bound in 1973, the book was not published until 1975.

About fifty copies were recased in marbled paper over boards by Gray Parrot in 1987.

In 1971 Grossman Publishers, New York, issued a trade edition of the book.

C.B. Brown, our first professional writer, whose gothic novels the printer had avidly read, had also written the first American book supporting the rights of women, never printed in its entirety until this edition. The discovery of this text was by accident, in the memoirs of a rare book dealer [it is extraordinary how boring these memoirs of an exciting trade tend to be]. Under the guiding aegis of Sidney Kaplan the complete work was assembled. It was edited by Lee Edwards & was an innovative & contributive addition to the subject. A popular edition was issued based on the Gehenna book.

68 (67) · TIRESIAS

T ‖ IRE ‖ SIAS ‖ ALFRED LORD TENNYSON [lines 1-3 in red] With 5 etchings by LB.

7 x 5. 22 leaves, untrimmed.

CONTENTS: 3 blank leaves; (1) blank; (2) frontispiece; (3) title page; (5) dedication; (7-24) text & etchings; (25) pressmark XIX; (27) colophon; 5 blank leaves.

COLOPHON: "Fifty copies of Tiresias have been printed at the Gehenna Press, Northampton, Massachusetts, in Centaur type on Fabriano paper. The pressman was Harold McGrath. The word Tiresias on the title page was engraved on boxwood by John E. Benson, and is printed here from the block. The etchings were printed by Annie Harris and John Keith in Northampton. The edition was bound by Arno Werner of Pittsfield, Mass. This is copy   Etchings by Leonard Baskin." Colophon signed &

numbered by LB.

Bound in full vellum & laid into a vellum & cloth traycase.
About half of the edition was destroyed by water damage at the
press in 1970.

*It was not Tennyson but Tiresias, the male–female archaic know-it-all that really interested me &
caused the poem to be printed. I had made a large sculpture of Tiresias, had to deal with his head turned
backwards in Dante, was oddly attracted to him & could not resist reprinting this relatively little known
poem. I thus had the possibility of doing several small & very hirsute etchings of him & in color the
copulating snakes whose secret procreative activities he penetrated to the vast annoyance of Artemis—
the cause of Tiresias' sexual change. The book is noteworthy for its title page, enhanced by a woodengraving of the title by John E. Benson, probably the world's finest living lapidarian, a great stone-
cutter in a great tradition.*

1971

69 (68) · ROMEYN DE HOOGHE

R ‖ *ROMEYN DE HOOGHE* ‖ *TO THE BURGERMASTERS
OF HAARLEM* ‖ [first line a calligraphic *"R"* printed from a line
cut, in red]

With a wood engraving by LB.

8½ x 5½. 8 leaves, untrimmed. Printed in red & black.

CONTENTS: 1 blank leaf; (1) wood engraving; (3) title page;
(5–9) text; (11) colophon; 1 blank leaf.

COLOPHON: *"One hundred copies printed at the Gehenna Press during
the summer of 1971. The letter now first printed in English is taken from
A. van der Willigen Pz., Geschiedkundige Aanteekeningen over
Haarlemsche Schilders, Haarlem, 1866. The paper is Amalfi. Harold
McGrath is the pressman. The type is Cancelleresca Bastarda, designed by
Jan van Krimpen & appropriately cast in Haarlem. The great R was made
by John E. Benson of Newport. The portrait of Romeyn de Hooghe was
engraved by Leonard Baskin & printed from the block. All copies carry a
signed additional impression printed on Japanese paper. This is copy   "*
Colophon signed & numbered by LB in most copies.

Bound in marbled paper, made by Peter Franck, over thin boards,
with a paper label on the front cover. The additional impression of
the wood engraving is laid in loosely.

4-page prospectus issued.

This booklet is a further display, although covert, of van Krimpen's Cancelleresca Bastarda type which the press kept buying. It is typographically noteworthy for exploiting the book's content, a letter, to show every ligature, swash-form & connected letter that van Krimpen had devised for his beautiful type. It is remarkably calligraphic in feeling as van Krimpen intended. R. de Hooghe was, in Otto Benesch's words, "the greatest Dutch 17th-Century etcher after Rembrandt," & I had gathered a large collection of books & broadsides illustrated by him. The booklet is further distinguished by the magnificent large baroque 'R' which graces the title-page, the work of John E. Benson.

1972

70 (69) · ANASTATIC PRINTING

· E · A · POE · ‖ ANASTATIC ‖ PRINTING ‖ [etching tipped-on]
[line 1 in red]
With a relief etching by LB.
8 ½ x 6. 12 leaves, untrimmed.
CONTENTS: 2 blank leaves; (1) half title; (3) title page; (5-12) text;
(13) pressmark XXa; (15) colophon, with pressmark VI in green;
2 blank leaves.
COLOPHON: "This near-fantasy by E.A.P. appeared originally in
the *Broadway Journal*, April 12, 1845. Sixty copies have been non-
anastatically printed at The Gehenna Press in Northampton, the
work finished during the Spring of 1972. The portrait of Poe by
Leonard Baskin, on the title page, has been achieved anastically
["anastically" deleted with a rule, & corrected to *"anastatically"* in
red in the margin] (now called relief etching). Harold McGrath
was the pressman. The paper is Italian. This is copy number   "
Colophon numbered.
TYPE: Centaur & Arrighi; PAPER: Amalfi.
Bound by John Newman of Dublin in yellow cloth over boards &
enclosed in a slipcase covered with marbled paper.
Although it was printed in 1972, & bound in 1973, the book was not
published until 1975.

71 (70) · THE DRAWINGS OF JACOB DE GHEYN II

THE DRAWINGS OF JACOB DE GHEYN II ‖ BY J. RICH-
ARD JUDSON ‖ [drawing] ‖ THE GEHENNA PRESS ‖ NOR-
THAMPTON ‖ MCMLXXII [first line in red]

Gehenna Essays in Art, No. 3. With 112 reproductions of de Gheyn's drawings.

10 x 7. 78 leaves. Printed in red & black.

CONTENTS: 1 blank leaf; (3) series title; (5) title page; (6) dedication; (7) prefatory note; 9-39 text; 41-(45) notes; (47) part title, "THE PLATES"; (49) part title, "THE PLATES"; (51-153) plates; (155) colophon, with pressmark XII in red.

COLOPHON: "One hundred and fifty copies of this, the third volume of The Gehenna Essays in Art, have been printed at The Gehenna Press in Northampton, Massachusetts. The text has been set in Monotype Bembo. The pressman was Harold McGrath. The plates have been printed by The Meriden Gravure Company in Meriden, Connecticut. The paper is Lippi, handmade in Italy. This is copy number   " Colophon numbered.

Bound by John Newman of Dublin in blue Ingres over boards, with an imitation vellum spine.

One part title was printed at Gehenna, the other at Meriden.

Although it was printed in 1972, & bound in 1973, the book was not published until 1975.

In 1964, the press had published J. S. Held's brilliant "Rembrandt & the Book of Tobit" as the second volume in the series, Gehenna Essays in Art. Eight years later was issued this innovative text of J. R. Judson regarding the diverse, powerful, probing & provoking, consummate & altogether quite amazing drawings by Jacob de Gheyn II. The text betrays its art historical roots, but informs us about de Gheyn, the structure of his workings within the specifics of his Dutch ambience. Many drawings are reproduced by Meriden Gravure with zealous fealty to the originals, rendering, to a surprising degree, a sense of the drawings' actuality. The press perforce dropped the series as we received no further texts.

72 (71) · PETER

PETER

A memorial volume for Peter Boynton. With 4 photographs & a watercolor, reproduced by offset.

9¾ x 7¼. 50 leaves. Printed in red & black.

CONTENTS: 1 blank leaf; (1) half title; (2) frontispiece; (3) title page; (5-6) preface; 7-(91) text & illustrations; (93) colophon; 2 blank leaves.

COLOPHON: "One hundred & ten copies have been printed at The Gehenna Press in 1972. The Meriden Gravure Company have printed all the plates. The typeface is Monotype Bembo, the paper was made in western Massachusetts. Harold McGrath was the pressman. William Meridith's poem, from *Open Sea and Other Poems,* copyright 1958, A.A. Knopf. The first line of the poem on page 65 is by Wallace Stevens. The Greek on page 61 translates: They brought me the news of your death, O Herakleitos my friend, and I wept for you, remembering how often we two in talking put the sun to rest." Colophon signed by LB.
Bound by Robert Burlen of Boston in linen & dark blue paper over boards, with paper labels on the front cover & spine.
Laid in loosely is a 10 x 4¾ card on white or red stock, which reads: "This book was completed on May thirtieth, nineteen seventy-two. The frontispiece is taken from the bronze portrait done in the summer of nineteen seventy at Deer Isle, Maine, by Leonard Baskin . . . The labels were set and printed at the Gehenna Press. The compiler and editor was Arthur Wensinger. . ." The card also gives information about the illustrations, editing, & copyright.

73 (72) · TERMINALIA
TERMINALIA ‖ FROM OVIDS FASTI · TRANSLATED BY ‖ SIR JAMES FRAZER · EIGHT ETCHINGS ‖ BY LEONARD BASKIN · THE GEHENNA ‖ PRESS · NORTHAMPTON · MCMLXXII [first line in red]
Etchings signed & numbered by LB.
11½ x 8¼. 30 leaves, untrimmed.
CONTENTS: 2 blank leaves; (1) half title; (3) title page; (5-8) text, in English & Latin; (9) part title, *"The etchings"*; (11-25) etchings; (27) colophon; 14 blank leaves.
COLOPHON: "Thirty five copies of Terminalia have been printed at the Gehenna Press in Northampton, Massachusetts. The paper is Millbourn laid, a now obsolete English hand-made paper. Harold McGrath was the pressman. Bruce Chandler printed the copper-

plates in the etching room at the Gehenna Press. The work finished during the summer of 1972. This is copy number   '' Colophon signed & numbered by LB.

TYPE: Kenntonian, with title page in Centaur.

Copies 1–30 were for sale.

Bound by Arno Werner in full leather, & laid into a leather & marbled paper traycase.

Two prospectuses issued, one with one page, the other with four pages.

The book was not published until 1974.

One again discerns the interactive dynamics of collecting on the workings of the press. ''Terminalia'' is the inevitable result of the printer's small passion for terminal figures and herms; he is the proud owner of Sambin's terms as well as suites by Ducerceau, V. de Vries & Boisteau. The ''Terminalia'' was followed [1986] by ''Hermaika'' & a third collection of these figures in woodcut begins to make formulations in my mind.

1973
74 · TITUS ANDRONICUS

WILLIAM ‖ SHAKESPEARE ‖ TITUS ANDRONICUS ‖
ILLUSTRATED BY LEONARD BASKIN [line 3 in red]
The Gehenna Shakespeare, Vol. 1. With 12 etchings & 16 wood engravings.

20 x 13½. 68 leaves. Printed in red & black.

CONTENTS: 1 blank leaf; (1) series title; (3) blank; (4) frontispiece; (5) title page; (7) dramatis personae; (9–129) text & illustrations; (131) colophon, with pressmark XXVI in red; 1 blank leaf.

COLOPHON: "This, the first volume of The Gehenna Shakespeare, illustrated with etchings and woodengravings by Leonard Baskin, is printed on Gehenna–Shakespeare, a paper made for the edition at the Strathmore mills. The etchings were printed by Emiliano Sorini at the Bank Street Atelier. The wood engravings, from the blocks, and the letterpress, in Centaur types, were printed by Harold McGrath. The text is based on the Methuen Arden edition, J.C. Maxwell, editor. An especially bound edition of one hundred and fifty copies, numbered I to CL, carries an extra suite of the etchings, each signed by the artist. Two hundred and fifty copies are numbered 1 to 250. This is copy   " Colophon signed & numbered by LB.

PAPER: etchings on Rives.

The etchings are on pages (4), (21), (31), (39), (53), (59), (67), (71), (79), (87), (111) & (123).

The regular edition was bound gradually. The first batch was bound by Arno Werner, some copies in full leather, laid into a traycase, other copies in leather & marbled paper over boards. Additional copies were later bound by Gray Parrot in full cloth. The 150 special copies referred to in the colophon were never issued, but Kennedy Galleries, New York, issued an edition of 200 special portfolios; these consisted of loose signatures & a second signed suite of the etchings laid into a cloth-covered portfolio.

4-page prospectus issued.

The etchings were not printed by Sorini, but by Bruce Chandler, Herb Fox, & others.

75 · OTHELLO

WILLIAM ‖ SHAKESPEARE ‖ OTHELLO ‖ ILLUSTRATED BY LEONARD BASKIN [line 3 in red]

The Gehenna Shakespeare, Vol. 2. With 23 drawings, printed from line cuts, & 10 woodcuts.

20 x 13½. 88 leaves. Printed in red & black.

CONTENTS: 3 blank leaves; (1) series title; (3) title page; (5) dramatis personae; (7-159) text & illustrations; (161) colophon, with pressmark XXVI in red; 4 blank leaves.

COLOPHON: "This, the second volume of The Gehenna Shakespeare, illustrated with woodcuts and drawings by Leonard Baskin, is printed on Gehenna-Shakespeare, a paper made for this edition by the Strathmore mills. The woodcuts are printed from the blocks on Japanese paper. The letterpress, hand-set in Centaur type by Mackenzie & Harris of San Francisco, was printed by Harold McGrath. The text is based on the Methuen Arden edition, M.R. Ridley, editor. Four hundred copies were printed as follows: two hundred with an additional suite of the woodcuts, signed by the artist, available only from Kennedy Galleries in New York, are numbered 1-200. Two hundred bound copies signed by Leonard Baskin in the colophon, are numbered I-CC. The work achieved in the winter of mcmlxxiii. This is copy   '' Colophon signed & numbered by LB.

The woodcuts are on pages (11), (29), (49), (63), (67), (85), (103), (121), (139) & (157).

The regular edition was bound gradually. The first batch was bound by Arno Werner, some copies in full leather, laid into a traycase, other copies in leather & marbled paper over boards. Additional copies were later bound by Gray Parrot in full cloth. The Kennedy Galleries edition was laid unbound into a portfolio & boxed.

4-page prospectus issued.

Only 300 copies were in fact printed: the bound edition was limited to 100 copies, numbered I-C.

At this point, the press dropped into the pit labelled 'hubris typographicus.' We were siezed with the idiotic idea that we should print a folio-sized, illustrated, complete Shakespeare. Such a desire once installed is so consumptive of reason that the editor fell in with this august & harebrained scheme. When the press discovered that the making of a hand-made paper, equivalent to our old Amalfi, would overwhelm that small industry's capacity, an omen should have been read & understood & we should have abandoned the project. No! we pushed on, & drove ourselves into the deepest debt with no redemptive profit on any level. The press, behaving with a possessed grandeur, loftily commanded from the Strathmore mills a pure paper, which was called 'Gehenna-Shakespeare'. The San Francisco typesetters Mackenzie & Harris cast a mass of Centaur type in 30 point & proceeded then to hand-set Titus Andronicus, Othello & Lear. Bless the memory of the beneficent Col. Harris who travelled East to see if those Gehennians were sane & who allowed us an immense measure of time to pay for all that Thompson cast & hand-set type. The etchings for Titus Andronicus are weak & very poorly serve the strong typography, & to heap additional expense with wayward zeal the sixteen text drawings were woodengraved in Chicago by Sanders, the last reproductive woodengraving firm to practice in the U.S.A. Our texts were based on the Arden edition, & our only contribution is a Titus & Othello without any broken lines. For the Othello I cut a set of woodcuts which, I think, depict Othello moving into the Iagoan terror with believability. It was an expensive fiasco, the black text of Lear printed but wanting the directive reds imprinted, which I presume will, one day, be achieved.

1974

76 · THE COAT WITHOUT A SEAM

THE COAT WITHOUT A SEAM ‖ SIXTY POEMS ‖
1930-1972 ‖ STANLEY KUNITZ ‖ [drawing] [line 2 in red]
The Gehenna Poets, No. 1. With a drawing by LB, printed from
a line cut.
11¼ x 7¼. 62 leaves, untrimmed. Printed in red & black.
CONTENTS: 5 blank leaves; (1) series title; (3) title page; (5-6) contents; (7) part title, "I ‖ THE BURNING CLOUD ‖ 1930-1944";
9-28 text; (29) part title, "II ‖ THIS GARLAND, DANGER ‖
1945-1959"; 31-62 text; (63) part title, "III ‖ NEXT TO LAST
THINGS ‖ 1960-1972"; 65-96 text; (97) pressmark XIX in grey;
(99) colophon, wih pressmark XXVII in red; 7 blank leaves.
COLOPHON: "This book, limited to one hundred & fifty copies,
was printed at The Gehenna Press in Northampton, Massachusetts
in Centaur monotype on Amatruda, an Italian handmade paper.
The portrait of the poet was drawn by Leonard Baskin. Harold
McGrath was the pressman. Five copies, numbered I to V, have an
additional impression of the drawing signed by the artist. The
regular edition, bound in half vellum & decorated-paper over
boards, is numbered 1 to 145. The work was finished in March 1974.
All the poems except *The Knot* are from the poet's *Selected Poems
1928-1958* (1958) & *The Testing Tree* (1971) . . . This is copy   "
Colophon numbered & signed by Kunitz.
Bound by Gray Parrot. The regular edition was bound in vellum &
blue paper over boards. The special copies have two additional
blanks, one initial & one final, & so have a total of 64 leaves; these
copies were bound in full vellum.

77 · BIRDS & ANIMALS

BIRDS & ANIMALS
With 65 wood engravings, woodcuts & linoleum cuts by LB.
11½ x 14½, oblong. 134 leaves, untrimmed. Printed on rectos only
in various colors.

CONTENTS: 1 blank leaf; (1) title page; 1 blank leaf; (5-261) prints; (263) colophon; 1 blank leaf.

COLOPHON: "Fifty copies of this collection were printed from the blocks by Harold McGrath in the summer of 1974."

TYPE: Lutetia; PAPER: Troya.

Many of the blocks are reprinted from earlier Gehenna Press books.

Some copies were bound by Arno Werner, some by David Bourbeau & some by Gray Parrot.

1-page prospectus issued.

In a few copies, all the prints are signed by LB.

Two earlier editions of the book were printed, the first in 1972, the second earlier in 1974. These editions each consisted of only a few copies, similar in format to this one, but with varying numbers of prints. Both editions were bound by Arno Werner.

1975

78 · CONSIDERATIONS ON THE KEEPING OF NEGROES

SOME CONSIDERATIONS ON THE KEEPING ‖ OF NE-GROES ‖ 1754 ‖ CONSIDERATIONS ON THE KEEPING ‖ OF NEGROES ‖ 1762 ‖ [drawing] ‖ JOHN WOOLMAN 1732-1772

The Gehenna Tracts, No. 2. With an afterword by Frederick B. Tolles, & a drawing by LB, printed from a line cut.

8 x 5¾. 54 leaves, untrimmed. Printed in green, red & black.

CONTENTS: 4 blank leaves; (1) series title; (3) title page; (5) part title, "SOME ‖ CONSIDERATIONS ON ‖ THE KEEPING OF ‖ NEGROES..."; (7)-(9) introduction; 10-(28) text; (29) part title, "CONSIDERATIONS ‖ ON KEEPING NEGROES..."; (31)-(33) preface; (34)-(85) text; (87) part title, "AN AFTERWORD ON WOOLMAN & SLAVERY"; (89-93) afterword; (95) colophon, with pressmark XVIII in red; 2 blank leaves.

COLOPHON: *"Two hundred & fifty copies were printed at The Gehenna Press to memorialize the bicentennial of John Woolman's death in 1772.*

The texts follow the first editions. The portrait by Leonard Baskin is based on a drawing from memory by Robert Smith III. The types are Centaur & Arrighi, the paper Fabriano, the pressman Harold McGrath. Copies one to twenty carry an additional impression of the portrait, signed by the artist.
©1975. . ..*This is copy* ''Colophon numbered.
Bound by Gray Parrot in leather & marbled paper over boards.
Pages (89-96) were printed in 1975, the year in which the book was published; they are printed on blue Fabriano. The rest of the book was printed in early 1970, & is on white Fabriano. Hence the order of publication of the Gehenna Tracts, nos. 2 & 3.
In 1976 Grossman Publishers, New York, issued a trade edition of the book.

The Woolman was the third & last of The Gehenna Tracts. It serves, as do its predecessors, in making available [especially as this text was popularly reprinted from our edition] works which are difficult to readily obtain. This was Gehenna's second Woolman text; earlier it had issued a large broadside of a nightmare of Woolman's entitled "The Fox and the Cat"; the press' editor rescued it from the obscurity of earlier Quaker journals.

1976
79 ·DEMONS IMPS & FIENDS
·DEMONS · ‖ ·IMPS · ‖ & ‖ ·FIENDS · ‖ DRAWINGS BY LEONARD BASKIN ‖ THE GEHENNA PRESS ‖ MCMLXXVI [lines 1-4 & 7 in red; lines 1-4 within the mouth of a drawing of a fiend]
With 19 drawings, printed from line cuts in red & black.
11 ½ x 8. 32 leaves, untrimmed. Printed on rectos only.
CONTENTS: 6 blank leaves; (1) title page; (3) quotation from St. Bernard of Clairvaux; (5-39) drawings; (41) colophon, with pressmark XXVIII; 5 blank leaves.
COLOPHON: "450 copies of this book were printed on various interesting papers during the autumn of 1976. The pressman was Harold McGrath. This is copy number '' Colophon numbered.
TYPE: Lutetia.
Bound by Gray Parrot in marbled paper over boards.
1-page prospectus issued.

1981

TED HUGHES ‖ A ‖ PRIMER ‖ OF ‖ BIRDS ‖ WOODCUTS
BY ‖ LEONARD BASKIN ‖ THE ‖ GEHENNA ‖ PRESS ‖ 19 · 81
[line 5 in red]
With 6 woodcuts, one printed in color from 7 blocks.
10¾ x 5¾. 24 leaves, untrimmed. Printed in red & black.
CONTENTS: (1) half title; (3) title page; (5) dedicatory poem; (7-41)
text & woodcuts; (43) colophon, with pressmark XXIX; 2 blank
leaves.
COLOPHON: "Two hundred and fifty copies of this book were
printed at The Gehenna Press, Lurley in Devon. The woodcuts
were printed from the blocks; the paper is Dover, handmade at
Maidstone, Kent, these copies are signed by the poet and the artist
and are numbered one to two hundred twenty five. Twenty five
copies have an additional suite of the woodcuts printed on a
Japanese paper, signed and numbered I–XXV by the artist. The
work was achieved on the press' nineteenth century Columbian
and finished during June MCMLXXXI. This is copy number   "
Colophon numbered & signed by LB & Hughes.
TYPE: Perpetua.
The woodcuts are on pages (11), (17), (23), (27), (33) & (41).
Bound by Nicholas Abrams. Copies 1–225 are bound in marbled
paper over boards, with paper labels on the front cover & spine;
copies I–XXV are bound in leather & paper over boards.
4-page prospectus, not printed at The Gehenna Press, issued.

*Five years elapsed before the Gehenna imprint reappeared. The printer & his family, in what seemed
like perpetuity, moved from Northampton to Devon, England & from the physical apparat of Gehenna. The press equipment was handed over to Harold McGrath for one dollar & one had hoped that a
fine jobbing office would develop. It was a farewell to a private printing means & to making books [with
the exception of the perplexing Shakespeare] with deep concern for content, with endless care for
typographic aptness & stylistic coherence & accompanied where likely with graphic works from many
hands. Within those years, with ever enveloping age & relative isolation in a remote Devonshire hamlet
[ie, no censoring editorial presence] the turn was inward & ego-fulfilling; the model had become
the 'Livres de Peintres'. The newer Gehenna books, after the somewhat backwards looking 'Primer of*

Birds,' have become less socially cogent in text but richer as object, fuller in artistry, & other artists were not invited to participate [there were & doubtless will continue to be exceptions to all of this.] The press had become for me, in the fifth decade of its existence, an extended preserve for my ever more engaged graphic enterprise. And the means had been discovered whereby the press stopped losing money. In 1985 Kenneth Shure had become the business agent for Gehenna & in whose understanding & participative hands the press has prospered. One of the outer sheds at Lurley came to be appointed with the stuff of printing & by 1981 a small office was established. Its equipment consisted of a large Columbian press, a medium sized Albion & a table-top Albion which had belonged to Bruce Rogers, & a stone, type & cases. I was determined to learn to print by hand so that I could print on dampened paper, laying open the fiber of the paper & allowing the metal types to achieve greater acuity with less ink. The press had in 1954 printed as a broadside 'Pike,' a poem of Ted Hughes [the second item in his bibliography]; that publication occurred at the beginning of a relationship that has deepened & ripened, indeed, it was Hughes' presence in Devon that tempted us there. We had collaborated on diverse books, commercial & private press publications, but never one for Gehenna. Proximity [we lived twenty miles from one another] & renewed intensity in our friendship led inevitably to the manuscript of "A Primer of Birds", a penetrating Hughesian incursion into avian disparity, splendor & fancy. I cut a number of concomitant woodcuts, had the poems set in Monotype Perpetua [in rather too small a size], acquired several reams of Dover, a handmade English paper & invited Bruce Chandler of The Heron Press, Boston, to come & teach us the mysteries of handprinting [which are heavily vested in the inking] & Gehenna was again underway. D.R. Wakefield who had been assisting me in mould making & other sculptural needs was endowed with vast capacities for mastery in matters technical. He quickly absorbed my scant technical knowledge & the considerable amount more of Chandler. His tendency toward virtuosity in understanding, performance & flair was breathtaking. Thus was Wakefield installed as compositor, pressman, & etching printer.

1982

81 · A GEHENNA ALPHABET

A GEHENNA ‖ ALPHABET ‖ THE DRAWINGS BY
LEONARD ‖ BASKIN WITH APHORISMS & POEMS ‖ BY
SIDNEY KAPLAN THE GEHENNA PRESS [line 2 in red]
With 26 drawings, printed from line cuts.

9 x 6½. 38 leaves, untrimmed. Printed in various colors.

CONTENTS: 2 blank leaves; (1) half title; (3) title page; (5) epigraphs; (6-57) text & drawings; (59) pressmark XXX; (61) errata; (63) colophon, with pressmark XXIX in red; 4 blank leaves.

COLOPHON: "One hundred & ten copies of this book have been printed on the Columbian hand-press at The Gehenna Press, Lurley, Devon, during the late spring of 1982. The papers are hand made at Maidstone, Kent. The copies are numbered 1-89. Twenty-one copies have an additional impression of the coloured

woodengraving printed from six blocks on Japanese paper; these are signed & lettered A–U by Leonard Baskin. All copies are signed by the artist. This is copy number,   " Colophon signed & numbered by LB & Sidney Kaplan.
TYPE: Caslon.
Bound by Gray Parrot in white paper over boards, and enclosed in a slipcase covered with marbled paper.
Very few copies were available; most of the edition remains unissued.

1983

82 · DIPTERA

DIPTERA ‖ A ‖ BOOK OF FLIES ‖ & ‖ OTHER INSECTS ‖ [3⅜-inch rule] ‖ ETCHINGS BY LEONARD BASKIN ‖ NOTE BY JOSE YGLESIAS ‖ THE GEHENNA PRESS ‖ MCMLXXXIII [first line in red]
With 37 etchings, printed in various colors, signed & numbered by LB.
11¾ x 8. 50 leaves, untrimmed. Tissue guards bound in.
CONTENTS: 4 blank leaves; (1) title page; (3–6) note; (7) list of etchings; 1 blank leaf; (11–45) etchings; 2 blank leaves; (51–81) etchings; (83) colophon, with pressmark XXXI touched with red & green watercolor; 4 blank leaves.
COLOPHON: *"Forty five copies of Diptera were printed at the Gehenna Press. The etchings were printed from the original plates on divers English hand-made papers. The edition is arranged as follows: copies numbered 1-5, have a second signed suite of the etchings, differentially printed; these copies also contain a watercolor drawing & one of the etched plates, lightly cancelled. Ten copies, numbered 6-15, have a second signed set of the etchings, printed as above on different papers & in variant colors. Thirty copies forming the regular edition are numbered 16-45. All copies have some watercolor in-painting. The work was completed during the spring of 1983. This is copy number* " Colophon signed & numbered by LB.
TYPE: Perpetua.

The sewn signatures are enclosed in a full leather chemise, & laid into a leather & marbled paper traycase, by Gray Parrot. The signatures are made up of the four initial blanks, pages 1-8, pages 9-48 & pages 49-92. The second suite in copies 1-15 makes up an additional two signatures, identical in format to the third & fourth signatures, but lacking the colophon. In copies 1-5, the watercolor is in a passepartout & the plate is in a well in the bottom of the traycase.

4-page prospectus issued.

My interest in the structural might & glory & performing magic of insects was only slightly exposed in 'Horned Beetles', & Diptera was, I think, inevitable. My friend, the superb American novelist Jose Yglesias, wrote a witty & delightfully arch introduction to this book mainly dealing with flies. Color is used with new but timid vigor, rising in one or two of the etchings to aver their colorful presences with notable insistence. Here too is a formulation that is invariably repeated, an interesting or beguiling subject, an introduction followed by a set of prints. This is an old formula, there are many Sixteenth Century books organized in this way.

83 · UNKNOWN DUTCH ARTISTS

VNKNOWN ‖ DVTCH ‖ ARTISTS ‖ *ETCHINGS AND BIOGRAPHICAL NOTICES ‖ BY LEONARD BASKIN THE EREMITE PRESS* [line 3 in red]

With 12 etchings, printed in various colors, signed & numbered by LB.

11¾ x 8¼. 18 leaves, untrimmed. Printed on rectos only. Tissue guards bound in.

CONTENTS: 1 blank leaf; (1) title page; (3-19) text & etchings; 1 blank stub; (23-29) text & etchings; (31) colophon, with "E P" in red; 1 blank leaf.

COLOPHON: *"Seventeen copies of this book were printed at the Eremite Press; the work finished early summer of 1983. The edition is arranged as follows: the etchings, in three copies, are touched in color by the artist, and are numbered 1-3. The subsequent fourteen copies are numbered 4-17. The presswork by D. R. Wakefield. The work printed on various English, hand-made papers. This is copy   "* Colophon signed & numbered by LB.

TYPE: Cancelleresca Bastarda & Perpetua.

Sewn into blue wrappers, with *UNKNOWN DUTCH ARTISTS* in red & a large ornament in black printed on the front cover.

This delicious jeu d'esprit was a proving-ground, the means by which we attained mastery over the hand-press. Its delicate assault on sensibility is vested in the unexpectedness of the book's mise-en-page [it is a paradigm for the 'Icones' of 1988.] Color, Fuseli's 'coy mistress', had been asserting itself in drawings & watercolors & now the printer's declared commitment to black & white was being undermined by color's blandishments & here is further praxis for forthcoming books. Thus, "Unknown Dutch Artists," although beset with whimsy & trimmed with irony, was of consequent importance in determining the appearance & attitude of many later Gehenna Press books.

1985

84 · MOKOMAKI

MOKOMAKI ‖ thirteen etchings ‖ of shrunken & tattooed ‖ Maori heads ‖ by ‖ Leonard Baskin ‖ & ‖ three poems ‖ by ‖ Ted Hughes [type within an arrangement of horizontal & vertical rules in red]

With 14 etchings, printed in various colors, signed by LB.

15 x 11. 35 leaves, untrimmed. Printed on rectos only. Tissue guards bound in.

CONTENTS: 4 blank leaves; (1) etched half title; (3) title page; (5-9) text; (11) part title, *"MOKOMAKI"*; (13-37) etchings; (39) colophon, with pressmark XXXII in red; 11 blanks.

COLOPHON: *"Fifty copies of Mokomaki were printed & issued during 1985 by The Eremite Press, Leeds, Massachusetts. The etchings were printed from the original plates on a variety of hand-made papers by Bruce Chandler. The type matter was printed photo-lithographically by Gail Alt and Lou Bannister at Amherst. The binding is by Gray Parrot of Easthampton. The edition is arranged as follows: copies numbered one to ten have a second set of the etchings printed on other papers & in different colors. The remainder of the edition is numbered eleven to fifty. This is copy number   "* Colophon signed & numbered by LB.

TYPE: a debased form of Palatino.

Copies 1-10 also contain an original drawing & one of the cancelled plates. They are bound in full leather, with the second set of etchings, and the drawing in a passepartout, enclosed in a full vellum chemise. The whole is laid into a leather & marbled paper traycase. The plate is in a well in the bottom of the traycase. Copies 11-50 are bound in full vellum, & laid into a leather & marbled paper traycase.

4-page prospectus issued.

A few sets of the etchings were printed on vellum.

The rich ethnological collections of the Brooklyn Museum had entranced me as a child when I paid them intense & long attendance. It was the works of the Northwest peoples & of the Maori that trapped my sharpest notice. I was overwhelmed by the fierce power locked in the totemic forms & of the ornamented power preserved in the Maori carvings. When, one day, at an antiquarian bookfair, I bought a book by a doubtlessly mad English Major-General on the tattooed, severed & mummified heads of Maori warriors, childish memories mingled with the book's extraordinary images & 'Mokomaki' ensued. Ted Hughes contributed three prefatory poems.

1986

85 · HERMAIKA

HERMAIKA ‖ HERMAIKA ‖ HERMAIKA ‖ HERMAIKA ‖ TWENTY ‖ EIGHT ‖ DRAWINGS & ‖ A WOODCUT ‖ BY LEONARD ‖ BASKIN ‖ [5⅞-inch rule] ‖ · THE EREMITE PRESS · 1986 · [line 4 in red; lines 1-10 within a large "H"]

14¾ x 11. 38 leaves, untrimmed. Printed on rectos only.

CONTENTS: 1 blank leaf; (1) half title; (3) title page; (5) note by LB; (7-61) drawings; (63) woodcut; (65) colophon; (67) pressmark XXXII in red; 3 blank leaves.

COLOPHON: "Seventy Five copies of Hermaika were printed during the summer of 1986. The work was achieved photo-lithographically by Gail Alt & Roberta Bannister at the Oxbow Press, Amherst. The woodcut was printed from the block by Daniel Keleher at the Wild · Carrot Letterpress, Hadley. The Binding was executed by David Bourbeau, Easthampton. The edition is arranged as follows: Copies 1-20 have a second impression of the woodcut hand painted by Leonard Baskin. Copies 21-75 have a single impression of the woodcut signed by the artist. This is copy number   " Colophon signed & numbered by LB.

TYPE: a debased form of Palatino; PAPER: Arches, Fabriano Ingres & Magnani; woodcut on Hosho; second impression on Barcham Green.

Bound in orange & brown paste paper over boards, & laid into a brown cloth traycase. In copies 1-20, the second impression of the woodcut is bound between (64) & (65), and there is an additional final blank; thus, the book has 40 leaves, not 38.

There is a prejudice abroad that dislikes, indeed abhors offset printing. The prejudiced cognoscenti pronounce the gospel that no typographic excellence can be achieved by photo-lithographic means. This is utter nonsense, particularly so since the availablity of the purest of Monotype faces to digital composition. There should be no suggestion of exclusivity of means, although the economics of contemporary printing has reduced printing from metal to a species of eccentricity, the concern & interest of fewer & fewer printers. The great typefounders, Klingspor, Enschedé, A.T.F., etc. have closed or lapsed into historical & technical museums. Digital composition can set types closer & lighter than the wildest metallic kerning. And in the hands of a sensitive pressperson, & with good black inks & fine papers, & with reasonable quotients of time & attention, the most beautiful of results are attainable. See, in Hermaika, the fidelity to the drawings in these reproductions by Gail Alt & Roberta Bannister of the Oxbow Press, Amherst, Mass., is remarkable. The subtleties in the drawings, the great varieties of tone & texture, are rendered with brilliant exactitude, the offsetters having at their behest the device of putting the sheets through the press two or even three times, enriching, deepening, enhancing the darks, the middle elusive hues & the lightest tonalities. The title means a collection of Herms; see the note to 'Terminalia' where I discuss my interest in these objects. The type in 'Hermaika' is, I fear, a distorted version of Palatino; Oxbow has since acquired a disc of purest Bembo, used in this catalogue.

1988

86 · ICONES LIBRORUM ARTIFICES

·ICONES· ‖ ·LIBRORVM· ‖ ·ARTIFICES· ‖ ·BEING ACT-VAL· PVTATIVE· ‖ FVGATIVE & FANTASTICAL ‖ POR-TRAITS OF ENGRAVERS· ‖ ILLVSTRATORS & BINDERS· ‖ ·ETCHINGS AND NOTES BY ‖ LEONARD BASKIN· ‖ ·THE GEHENNA PRESS· ‖ ·MCMLXXXVIII· [lines 1-3 & 10: text in red, dots in black; type within an arrangement of horizontal & vertical rules]

With 32 etchings, printed in various colors, signed & numbered by LB.

16 x 11¼. 48 leaves, untrimmed. Printed in italic on rectos only. Tissue guards bound in.

CONTENTS: 5 blank leaves; (1) title page; (3-73) etchings & notes; (75) colophon, with pressmark XXXIII in red; 5 blank leaves.

COLOPHON: *"Forty copies of Icones Librorum Artifices have been printed by The Gehenna Press, Leeds, Mass^etts; The work finished in April, 1988. Composition and presswork are by Arthur Larson assisted by K Howat. The etchings were printed from the original coppers by D. R. Wakefield of Howden, England. The edition is arranged as follows: three copies, numbered 1-3, have a second suite of the etchings, 3 watercolors & 2 copperplates; five copies, numbered 4-8, have the second suite and a copperplate; copies bearing numbers 9-40 comprise the regular edition. This is number   "* Colophon signed & numbered by LB.

TYPE: Arrighi; PAPER: divers English handmade papers.

Bound by Gray Parrot. Copies 1-8 are bound in full leather, with the second suite in a cloth folder, the watercolors each in a passepartout, and the plates each in a well in the bottom of the leather & cloth traycase into which the whole is laid. Copies 9-40 are bound in leather & marbled paper over boards, and laid into a leather & cloth traycase.

'Icones' has been called the masterwork of the press. It may be, I cannot say. The book is a flowering & a fulfilling resolution of elements but tentatively used in precedent books. Color emblazons the pages of 'Icones'; in printing etchings the press was becoming very proficient [especially with the advent of Michael Kuch] in the uses of color. It uses overlays, with & without stencilled definition & it makes great use of á la poupée & other coloring devices. The portraits are of various sizes & differing contours & they with the shaped texts together form new configurations, framing an odd geometry of humanist book-workers. The difficult & complex composition & its perfect subsequent printing was achieved by Arthur Larson of Hadley, Mass. The etchings were flawlessly printed in England by D.R. Wakefield.

87 · TWELVE SCULPTORS

TWELVE SCVLPTORS ‖ A BOOK OF MONOTYPES ‖ WITH SHORT NOTES ‖ ON THE MONOTYPES & ‖ THE SCVLPTORS BY ‖ LEONARD BASKIN ‖ THE ‖ EREMITE ‖ PRESS ‖ 1988 ‖ RVSH ‖ WARD ‖ SAINT-GAVDENS ‖ RIMMER ‖ FRENCH ‖ MACMONNIES ‖ VONNOH ‖ FLANAGAN ‖ NADELMAN ‖ LACHAISE ‖ O'CONNOR ‖ ·L·B· [first line in red; lines 2-10 & 11-22 in two columns, with a 2¼-inch vertical red rule separating them]

With 12 monotypes by LB.

11¼ x 8¼. 36 leaves, untrimmed. Printed in red & black. Tissue guards bound in.

CONTENTS: 4 blank leaves; (1) title page; (3) dedication; (5-11) text, part I; (13-24) text, part II; 1 blank leaf; (27-49) monotypes; (51) colophon, with pressmark XXXIV; 6 blank leaves.

COLOPHON: "Twentyfive copies of · Twelve Sculptors · were made at the Eremite Press, Leeds, Mass. The monotypes were printed by the artist with the assistance of Peter Bogardus. The Spectrum types were cast by Harold Berliner's Typefoundry & printed by Arthur Larson. The work was finished during the long, very hot Summer of 1988. This is copy number   " Colophon signed & numbered by LB.

PAPER: text on Magnani; monotypes on various hand-made & mould-made papers.

Bound by Gray Parrot in full vellum, and laid into a vellum & paste paper traycase.

It was the singularity of the monotype & the wondrous richness of its color when impressed & compacted onto the surface of pure paper that impelled me to devise two books with the particularity of the monotype extended, to allow two small editions. The 'Twelve Sculptors' is an homage, furthering my avowed tendency toward the making of iconologias. In the longish introductory notice I explained the techniques by which the number of monotypic impressions can be extended. The second book, 'Recollected Fragments of Ornament & Grotesque', expresses my seemingly endless interest in ornaments, reinforced by recent collecting of arabesque, moresque & grotesque prints; the collecting passion has irrepressibly erupted into several Gehenna books. These recollections were triggered by two summers spent at Florence & its wealth of near ubiquitous architectural ornament.

88 · ONE GERMAN DEAD

ONE GERMAN DEAD ‖ BY ‖ JOSE YGLESIAS ‖ WITH A ‖ COMPOSITE PORTRAIT ‖ OF ‖ JOSE YGLESIAS ‖ BY ‖ LEONARD BASKIN ‖ THE EREMITE PRESS · 1988 [first line in red]

With a signed etching by LB.

9¾ x 5¾. 32 leaves.

CONTENTS: 3 blank leaves; (1) half title; (3) title page; (5) etching, with tissue guard bound in; (7-52) text; (53) colophon, with pressmark XXXII; 2 blank leaves.

COLOPHON: "One hundred and ten copies of 'One German Dead' were printed by The Eremite Press of Leeds, Mass. The work was achieved during the summer of 1988 by the Oxbow Press of Amherst, Mass. The etchings were printed from the copperplates. Copies numbered 1-15 have a second impression of the composite portrait printed on different papers & one colored by the artist. All copies are signed by the artist. This is copy number   " Colophon numbered and signed by Yglesias.

TYPE: a debased form of Palatino; PAPER: Gutenberg.
Bound by Gray Parrot. Copies 1-15 bound in leather & paste paper over boards & laid into a cloth traycase, with the two additional impressions in a cloth folder. Copies 16–115 bound in paste paper over boards.

4-page prospectus issued [in conjunction with *GYPSY & OTHER POEMS.*]

89 · RECOLLECTED FRAGMENTS OF ORNAMENT & GROTESQUE

[etching] ‖ [7½-inch rule, in red] ‖ · *RECOLLECTED FRAG-MENTS OF ORNAMENT & GROTESQUE · A BOOK OF MONOTYPES BY LEONARD BASKIN ·*
With 18 signed monotypes, an etching & an essay by LB.
15¾ x 14½. 34 leaves, untrimmed. Printed in italic. Tissue guards bound in.

CONTENTS: 4 blank leaves; (1) title page; (3-9) text; (11-45) mono-types; (47) colophon, with pressmark XXXV; 6 blank leaves.

COLOPHON: "Fourteen copies of 'Recollected Fragments of Orna-ment & Grotesque' have been printed by the Eremite Press of Leeds, Mass^etts. The monotypes were printed by the artist with the assistance of Peter Bogardus. The letterpress was printed by Arthur Larson of Hadley, Mass. The prints are signed & the copies numbered by the artist. Ten copies only are for sale. The work achieved during the late summer & autumn of 1988. This is copy number   " Colophon signed & numbered by LB.

TYPE: Arrighi; PAPER: text on Magnani; monotypes on various papers, including papers by Fabriano & Barcham Green. Bound by Gray Parrot in full leather, and laid into a leather & paste paper traycase.

90 · SOME MARBLED PAPERS BY GRAY PARROT

SOME MARBLED PAPERS ‖ BY GRAY PARROT ‖ 1988
Mounted samples of papers marbled by Gray Parrot, with a prefatory note by the marbler.
12¼ x 12½, oblong. 94 leaves. Printed in italic, in red & black.
CONTENTS: 4 blank leaves; (1) title page; (3-6) note; 1 blank leaf; (9-161) marbled papers; 1 blank leaf; (165) colophon, with press-mark XXXV; 7 blank leaves.
COLOPHON: *"Thirty-two copies of this book have been made at the Eremite Press, Leeds, Mass^etts. The typeface is Arrighi, the letterpress printed by Arthur Larson. The whole arranged by Leonard Baskin. Mcmlxxxviii. This is copy number   "* Colophon numbered & signed by Parrot & LB.
PAPER: Magnani.
Bound by Gray Parrot in leather & marbled paper over boards, and laid into a leather, marbled paper & cloth traycase.

91 · IRISES

A BOOK OF ETCHINGS ‖ IRISES ‖ LEONARD BASKIN
[the whole within an ornamental border; lines 1 & 3 in red; line 2 & the border printed from an etched plate]
With 17 etchings, each printed in black & white, & then in color. Some of the plates are printed three or four times, in different color variations. Each impression, or group of impressions, is signed & numbered by LB.
13¼ x 12. 40 leaves, untrimmed. Printed in italic on rectos only. Tissue guards bound in.
CONTENTS: 2 blank leaves; (1) title page; (3-69) etchings; (71) colophon, with pressmark XXXVI; 2 blank leaves.
COLOPHON: *"Thirty-five copies of Irises were achieved by The Eremite*

Press during the Spring & Winter of 1988. This is copy number ''
Colophon signed & numbered by LB.
TYPE: Arrighi; PAPER: various papers by Fabriano & Barcham
Green.
Bound by Gray Parrot in full leather & laid into a leather & cloth
traycase.

*'Irises' exists as a book primarily because it is beautifully bound by Gray Parrot in full citron or peacock
blue oasis niger. Elements of rhythm, movement & cadence are induced, indeed, insisted upon, because
the irises are fixed in sequence & ordered & inflexibly so, they are in bound rigor. For influence, one must
look at & consider the vast numbers of sets of engravings by divers artists, such as the de Brys, Galles,
Sadelars, Wierixes, Collaerts, De Passes, della Bella & Callot, which more often than not are
bound-up.*

1989

92 · FANCIES, BIZARRERIES & ORNAMENTED GROTESQUES

*FANCIES ‖ BIZARRERIES ‖ & ‖ ORNAMENTED ‖
GROTESQUES ‖ Etchings by ‖ Leonard Baskin ‖ With an essay on ‖
· The Arabesque · ‖ by ‖ Johann Wolfgang von Goethe ‖ The Eremite
Press ‖ Leeds ‖ 1989* [lines 1–2, 4–5 & 14 & the text on line 9 in red]
With 24 etchings, printed in various colors, signed & numbered by
LB. The essay was translated by Alex Page.
15¾ x 10½. 38 leaves, untrimmed. Printed in red & black. Tissue
guards bound in.
CONTENTS: 2 blank leaves; (1) title page; (3–12) text; 1 blank leaf;
(15–61) etchings; (63) colophon, with pressmark XXXIV in red;
4 blank leaves.
COLOPHON: "Thirty-five copies of 'Fancies, Bizarreries & Ornamented Grotesques' were achieved by The Eremite Press in the
very early spring of 1989. The etchings were printed from the
original coppers by D. R. Wakefield of Howden, England. The
Bembo type was cast at Harold Berliner's Typefoundry & printed
by Arthur Larson. The edition is arranged as follows: copies numbered 1–3 have two extra suites, one hand-colored by the artist &
the other in different inks & on other papers; copies 4–8 have the
second suite of etchings; & copies 9–35 comprise the regular edi-

tion. This is number   '' Colophon signed & numbered by LB.
PAPER: various English hand made papers.
Bound by Gray Parrot. Copies 1-3 bound in full leather, with a
cloth folder to hold the two additional suites, & laid into a leather
& cloth traycase. Copies 4-8 not yet bound. Copies 9-35 bound in
leather & marbled paper over boards, & laid into a leather & cloth
traycase.
1-page prospectus issued.

*The collecting of ornaments has indubitably informed the making of this book's prints, not directly, but
by the influence being expressed in subtleties of nuance, pulse & tone. Ivins acutely noted that no artist
ever entirely invented an ornament print. The classic ideas, notions & designs find reformation & fresh
configuration in the etchings that jostle this book's pages. The book is further enriched by having as its
preface a hitherto untranslated essay by Goethe 'On the Arabesque.' Technically the book is a retreat
from the color adventures of 'Icones,' although it is not without its share of gaudy.*

93 · GYPSY & OTHER POEMS

GYPSY ‖ & OTHER POEMS ‖ JAMES BALDWIN ‖ THE
GEHENNA PRESS ‖ MCMLXXXIX [first line in red]
With an etching [6 etchings] signed & numbered by LB.
12 x 8¾. 28 leaves, untrimmed. Printed in red & black.
CONTENTS: 4 blank leaves; (1) half title; (3) title page; (5-24) text;
(25) part title, *"PORTRAIT OF JAMES BALDWIN ‖ BY
LEONARD BASKIN"*; (27) etching; (29) pressmark XXXVII
in red; (31) colophon; 8 blank leaves.
COLOPHON: "Three hundred & twenty-five copies of 'Gypsy &
Other Poems' were printed by The Gehenna Press during the
Spring of 1989. The poems are copyrighted by David Baldwin.
The special casting of Centaur was made by Harold Berliner's
Typefoundry at Nevada City, Calif. The presswork was achieved
at Wild Carrot Letterpress of Hadley, Mass. The etchings have
been printed from the copperplates. The edition is arranged as
follows: copies numbered 1-50 have a portfolio of etched portraits,
signed & numbered by the artist & are specially bound; copies
51-325 have a signed & numbered etched portrait. Six special
copies, 'hors d'edition', lettered a-f, contain an original copper & a

drawing. This is copy number   " Colophon signed & numbered by LB.

PAPER: Magnani.

Copies 1-50 & a-f bound by Daniel Gehnrich in leather & paste paper, made by Babette Gehnrich, over boards, and laid into a cloth traycase. In copies a-f, the drawing is in a cloth folder, and the copperplate is in a well in the bottom of the traycase. Copies 51-325 bound by Claudia Cohen in paste paper over boards.

Copies 1-50 & a-f have 27 leaves, not 28; their contents are as follows: 3 blank leaves; (1) half title; (3) title page; (5-24) text; (25) part title, *"PORTRAITS OF JAMES BALDWIN* ‖ *BY LEONARD BASKIN"*; (27-37) etchings; (39) pressmark XXXVII in red; (41) colophon; 3 blank leaves. The etchings have tissue guards bound in.

4-page prospectus issued [in conjunction with *ONE GERMAN DEAD*.]

Departing from its new preciosity, the press issued 'Gypsy', a book of unpublished poems by James Baldwin, a recent friend, who had been moved by the Othello woodcuts. The book that we discussed doing turned, alas, into a volume memorializing Baldwin. He died unexpectedly and prematurely. I etched six portraits of Baldwin from early manhood to the visage of his last years. 'Gypsy' hearkens to an older Gehenna modality, in that a large number of copies were produced & the text was important & printed in this instance for the first time. Thus, 'Gypsy' points in part to 'Capriccio' of the next year, that book representing to my mind an ideal of text & illustration.

94 · EFFLEURAGE

EFFLEURAGE ‖ ETCHINGS BY ‖ ANNA MARIA BAR-TOLINI ‖ INTRODUCTION BY ‖ MARIO GRAZIANO PARRI ‖ THE GEHENNA PRESS ‖ MCMLXXXIX [lines 1 & 6 in red]

With 20 etchings & 8 woodcuts, signed & numbered by Bartolini. 14 x 9¾. 36 leaves, untrimmed.

CONTENTS: 1 blank leaf; (1) half title; (3) title page; (5-11) introduction; (13-63) prints; (65) colophon, with pressmark XXXIV in red; 2 blank leaves.

COLOPHON: "Thirty-eight copies of *Effleurage* have been printed

by The Gehenna Press during the early winter of 1989. The etchings by Anna Maria Bartolini were printed at Florence, Italy. This
is copy number   " Colophon numbered.
TYPE: Spectrum; PAPER: Magnani, Fabriano & a rude Amalfi.
Bound by Kim O'Donnell in cloth & paste paper over boards &
laid into a cloth & paste paper traycase.

1990

95 · CAPRICCIO

CAPRICCIO ‖ POEMS BY ‖ TED HUGHES ‖ ENGRAVINGS
BY ‖ LEONARD ‖ BASKIN ‖ THE GEHENNA PRESS ‖
MCMXC [type surrounded by woodcut borders, below a 4-color
woodcut]
With 19 etchings, 6 woodcuts & a wood engraving, printed in
various colors, signed & numbered by LB [prints on (1), (3) & (85)
are not signed & numbered.]
20¼ x 13¾. 50 leaves, untrimmed.
CONTENTS: 4 blank leaves; (1) etched & letterpress half title; (3) title
page; (5-83) text & engravings; (85) colophon, with etching above
text; 3 blank leaves.
COLOPHON: "Fifty copies of Capriccio were issued in the unsettled
Spring of 1990. The papers throughout were handmade in Italy &
France. Jan van Krimpen's Spectrum types were supplied by the
Berliner Typefoundry at Nevada City, Ca. The composition &
printing of the letterpress was achieved by Arthur Larson & Daniel
Keleher of Hadley, Mass. The copperplates were printed by D. R.
Wakefield of Humberside, Eng^d and by Michael Kuch of Northampton, Ma. The edition is arranged as follows: ten copies, numbered 1-10 have a second suite of the engravings printed variously &
on different papers; these copies also contain a page of Ted Hughes'
manuscript & a drawing by Leonard Baskin; they also carry one of
the copperplates. Copies numbered 11-50 comprise the regular
edition. All copies are signed by the poet & the artist." Colophon
numbered & signed by Hughes & LB.

Bound by Gray Parrot in full leather, and laid into a leather & cloth traycase. In copies 1-10 there is also laid into the traycase a cloth folder, which contains the second suite, the drawing in a passepartout & the manuscript in a paper folder; these copies also have a well in the bottom of the traycase to hold the copperplate.
1-page prospectus issued.

Here, I believe, is Gehenna at its new & lavish best, a great text, new unpublished poems by Ted Hughes, buttressed by twenty six etchings & woodcuts. ''Capriccio'' is heavily equipped with a figured half-title & pictorial title-page unusual for Gehenna, where in general bastard titles are spare & title pages are adorned with a bit of ornament & a touch of color. The book is grandly large, a huge folio with a great cargo of illustration. The illustrations are hugely various, from full-page woodcuts to small, delicate etchings entailed with densities of detail, all held in consolidated severity by the stately ranks of the on-coming thirty point type. The poetry's setting is so continuous & monumental that it allows images of any size to lay-up against its bulk or be placed demurely away from its great massivity. Here is perfection & preciousness to a nicety. The letterpress was printed with the firmest finesse by Daniel Keleher of Hadley, Mass.

1991

96 · SIBYLS

[woodcut] ‖ SIBYLS ‖ A BOOK OF POEMS ‖ BY RUTH FAINLIGHT ‖ WOODCUTS ‖ BY LEONARD BASKIN ‖ THE GEHENNA PRESS ‖ MCMXCI
With 13 woodcuts. 12 are printed in color from as many as five blocks, and are signed & numbered by LB.
22½ x 15. 28 leaves, untrimmed.
CONTENTS: (1) half title; (3) title page; (5-51) text & woodcuts; (53) colophon, with pressmark XXXVIII in red & black; 1 blank leaf.
COLOPHON: "26 copies of Sibyls were issued in the warm winter of 1991. Handmade papers were used throughout. The type is van Krimpen's Spectrum cast & set at Golgonooza Letter Foundry. The woodcuts were printed in color by Arthur Larson, the letterpress by Daniel Keleher, both of Hadley, Mass. The edition is arranged as follows: eight copies, numbered 1-8, have an extra suite of woodcuts printed in black & white, an impression in color from an additional woodcut, a drawing by Leonard Baskin, and one of

the blocks. Eighteen copies, numbered 9–26, comprise the regular edition. This is copy nº   ″ Colophon numbered & signed by Fainlight & LB.

PAPER: Moulin du Gué; woodcuts on Hosho & Sekishu; second suite on Arches.

Not bound: enclosed in a cloth-covered chemise, and laid into a cloth traycase, by Gray Parrot. Copies 1–8 have a well in the bottom of the traycase to hold the woodblock.

1-page prospectus issued.

A few copies were bound by Gray Parrot in leather & cloth over boards. These copies have two additional blanks, one initial & one final, & so have a total of 30 leaves.

97 · GROTESQUES

·GROTESQVES· ‖ [fleuron in green] *ETCHINGS* ‖ *&* ‖ *A PANE-GYRICAL* ‖ *NOTE* ‖ *BY* ‖ *LEONARD BASKIN* ‖ ·‖ *THE GEHENNA PRESS* ‖ *MCMXCI* [fleuron in green] [text of line 1, & lines 8 & 10, in red]

With 48 etchings, printed in various colors. The 33 etchings that constitute the main body of the book are each signed & numbered by LB.

13 x 9¾. 46 leaves, untrimmed. Printed in italic.

CONTENTS: 1 blank leaf; (1) etched & letterpress half title; (3) title page; (5) epigraphs, with an etching above text; (7–14) note, with marginal etchings; (15) part title, "·*BIRDS*·"; (17–29) etchings; (31) part title, "·*IMPS*· ‖ *&* ‖ ·*PVNCHINELLOS*·"; (33–45) etchings; (47) part title, "·*ARABESQVES & MORESQVES*·"; (49–55) etchings; (57) part title, "·*INSECTS*·"; (59–69) etchings; (71) part title, "·*BEINGS*·"; (73–85) etchings; (87) colophon, with pressmark XXXIX; 1 blank leaf.

COLOPHON: *"Twenty-six copies of* Grotesques *were printed at The Gehenna Press; The work achieved at onset of deep Autumn, 1991. The etchings were printed from the copperplates by Michael Kuch. All of the color is printed. The letter-press was the work of Arthur Larson. The papers are hand made in France & Italy. The edition is arranged as follows: copies number 1-8 have a second suite of etchings, printed in different colors & on various papers. These copies carry an original copperplate and a drawing in color. Copies numbered 9-26 comprise the regular edition. Five copies, hors d'edition & hors de commerce are made for the printer & his collaborators & bear Roman numerals I-V. This is copy number* "Colophon signed & numbered by LB.

TYPE: Spectrum.

Bound by Gray Parrot, a few copies in marbled paper over boards, the rest in full vellum, all laid into a cloth traycase. In copies 1–8, the second suite is in a paper folder, & the drawing is in a passepartout; both are enclosed in a cloth-covered chemise, which is also laid into the traycase. The plate is in a well in the bottom of the traycase. 4-page prospectus issued.

Copies 1–3 also contain a suite of etchings that were not used in the final version of the book; these 19 etchings, printed on 17 sheets, are in a paper folder in the chemise with the second suite & the drawing.

WORKS IN PROGRESS

DEATH MASKS

Death Masks avidly interest me because they fall between the two stools of nature & of art. Not natural, because death has reorganized the formal structures of the face, and not art, because no artist's expressive intelligence has intervened in arranging the face, neither helpfully nor ruinously. This small book contains etchings of masks I have responded to, for one or another reason. They are rendered from reproductions in books, where, oddly, very few masks of women are represented. The poems are by a San Franciscan art dealer who has been writing verse for many years. It is the Germans who are most interested in death masks. The only original book in English is Hutton's 'Portraits in Plaster', published early in this century. Virginia & Leonard Woolf issued from their Hogarth Press an English translation of the great book by Berkhard 'Das Ewige Artlitz' [The Eternal Visage'].

JEWISH ARTISTS OF THE EARLY & LATE RENAISSANCE

In a manner very like 'Unknown Dutch Artists', this little hoax grants me a further measure of small portrait-making, however fictive the artists may be. It is a small phantasy, inventing & imagining early Jewish artists and their work which happily answer a number of exceedingly difficult art-historical problems. Such are the enriched benefits of invention, caprice's imaginative gift to reality. There is typographic play in the working of a form-binding cohesion between the etched portraits & their permutations & the shape-related geometry of the text. My son Hosea Baskin has achieved the compositional tasks [especially noteworthy is the mind and hand cracking work presented by Isaac Simon, trapped as he is in a double circle] & the printing on an Albion hand-press. The etchings were printed by Michael Kuch.

BROADSIDES

1952

B1 · THE GEHENNA PRESS

THE GEHENNA PRESS
Announcement of the beginning of the press, listing the first items to be printed.
22 x 9½. 1 sheet.
With pressmarks II & III in red.
COLOPHON: "E. & L. BASKIN 6 CASTLE Street WORCESTER, Mass."
TYPE: Caslon; PAPER: Atlantic Bond.
Some copies were also printed on Strathmore Artist, 19 x 12½, untrimmed.

B2 · JACK PLAIN DEALING

JACK PLAIN DEALING ‖ The Poor Mans Complaint ‖ Or The Sorrowful Lamentation Of Poor Plain-Dealing, ‖ At This Time Of Distress And Trouble. [first line printed from a woodcut; lines 2-4 in red]
With a woodcut by LB.
19 x 12½. 1 sheet, untrimmed. Printed in red & black.
COLOPHON: "The Gehenna Press E. & L. Baskin 1952"
TYPE: Artcraft Roman & Caslon; PAPER: buff Strathmore Artist.
About 50 copies printed.

B3 · EASTER 1916

easter 1916 ‖ William Butler Yeats [type in red]
With a 2-color woodcut by LB.
20½ x 24, oblong. 1 sheet, untrimmed. Printed in red & black.
COLOPHON: "E. & L. Baskin The Gehenna Press 6 Castle Street Worcester Massachusetts"
PAPER: green Ingres.
40 copies printed.
1-page prospectus issued.

B4 · A CANDLE

A CANDLE ‖ SIR JOHN SUCKLING
With a wood engraving by LB.
Varying sizes, from 9 x 5¼ to 13 x 10. 1 sheet, untrimmed.
COLOPHON: "E&L BASKIN THE GEHENNA PRESS 1952"
TYPE: Artcraft Roman; PAPER: some on Strathmore Pastelle, others
on Strathmore Text.
The wood engraving later appeared on page 9 of *THE TUNNING
OF ELYNOUR RUMMYNGE*.

1955

B5 · AS CONSEQUENT, ETC.

A Poem, AS CONSEQUENT, Etc. written by WALT WHIT-
MAN ‖ *issued to celebrate the publication of LEAVES OF GRASS in
1855. [AS CONSEQUENT, Etc.,* WALT WHITMAN, *LEAVES
OF GRASS,* & *1855* in red]
With a wood engraving by LB.
19 x 19½, oblong. 1 sheet. Printed in red & black.
COLOPHON: "Printed by E. & L. Baskin, and R. Warren, at The
Gehenna Press, Northampton, Mass. 1955"
TYPE: Ludlow Goudy Bold; PAPER: Flemish Book.
250 copies printed.
1-page prospectus issued.

1959

B6 · PIKE

PIKE A POEM BY TED HUGHES WOODCUT BY
ROBERT BIRMELIN [first word in red]
Woodcut printed in green & black.
21 x 16. 1 sheet, untrimmed. Printed in red & black.
COLOPHON: "200 COPIES PRINTED BY E. & L. BASKIN AND
RICHARD WARREN AT THE GEHENNA PRESS NORTH-
AMPTON MASSACHUSETTS 1959"
TYPE: Perpetua; PAPER: Shogun.
In some copies, the type is printed entirely in black.

1962

B7 · THIS TOO SHALL PASS AWAY

THIS TOO SHALL PASS AWAY
Quotations from Polybius, Marcus Aurelius, H. L. Mencken &
Goldsworthy Lowes Dickinson. With a Zodiacal woodcut.
15 x 5¼. 1 sheet, untrimmed. Printed in orange & black.
TYPE: Garamond; PAPER: Millbourn Book Laid.

B8 · ON THE NATURE OF INSPIRATION

WILLIAM MORRIS ‖ ON THE NATURE OF INSPIRA-
TION [type in red]
Text from H. Halliday Sparling's *The Kelmscott Press and William
Morris Master-Craftsman*. With a wood engraving by LB.
17 x 4½. 1 sheet, untrimmed. Printed in red & black.
COLOPHON: "ONE HUNDRED COPIES PRINTED AT THE
GEHENNA PRESS JUNE MCMLXII"
TYPE: Garamond; PAPER: various.

1964

B9 · JERUSALEM

WILLIAM BLAKE FROM *JERUSALEM*
8½ x 22, oblong. 1 sheet. Printed in red & black.
COLOPHON: "100 COPIES PRINTED AT THE GEHENNA
PRESS ON THE OCCASION OF THE VISIT OF THE
SOCIETY OF PRINTERS, BOSTON OCTOBER, 1964."
Colophon numbered.
TYPE: Bembo & Centaur; PAPER: Frankfurt.

c. 1964

B10 · THE FLOWERING OF THE HOUSE IS HOSPITALITY

The flowering of the house is Hospitality ‖ The singing of the
house is Serenity ‖ The halo of the house is Graciousness ‖ The
laurel wreath of the house is Contentment [text in a box of rules &
fleurons]
9½ x 11⅞, oblong. 1 sheet, untrimmed. Prnted in italic.

COLOPHON: [on verso] "Privately printed by Leonard Baskin at The Gehenna Press in a tiny edition of 15 copies of which this is number ." Colophon numbered.
TYPE: Bembo; PAPER: Frankfurt.

1967
B11 · THE EEMIS STANE
HUGH MACDIARMID *THE EEMIS STANE*
With a woodcut portrait of MacDiarmid, drawn by LB & cut by Takeshi Takahara.
23 x 13½. 1 sheet, untrimmed. Printed in red & black.
COLOPHON: *"Five hundred copies printed at The Gehenna Press at Northampton, Massachusetts, April 1967."*
TYPE: Bembo & Palatino; PAPER: 450 on Nideggen, 50 on Kochi. The copies on Kochi are signed by the artists.
1-page [folded] prospectus issued.

c. 1967
B12 · DICKENS
A quotation from Dickens in praise of the printer, with pressmark XXI in red.
10 x 4. 1 sheet, untrimmed. Printed in red & black.
TYPE: Centaur & Cancelleresca Bastarda; PAPER: Nideggen.

1969
B13 · A VOYAGE TO THE MOON
A VOYAGE TO THE MOON
A poem by Archibald MacLeish.
19 x 9½. 1 sheet. Printed in red, blue & black.
COLOPHON: *"850 copies printed at the Gehenna Press 1969"*
TYPE: Centaur; PAPER: a heavy Japanese paper.
12 copies were signed by MacLeish.
Much of the edition was destroyed by water damage at the press in 1970.

MELVILLE ON PIRANESI [in grey]
With the etched title page of Piranesi's *Carceri,* reproduced by offset.
24¼ x 17½. 2 leaves, untrimmed. Printed in red, grey & black.
CONTENTS: (1) title page; (2) mounted etching; (3) excerpt from
Melville's *Clarel;* (4) colophon.
COLOPHON: *"Twelve hundred copies of this broadside were printed at The
Gehenna Press & The Meriden Gravure Company in December 1969 for
the one hundred & fiftieth anniversary of the birth of Herman Melville."*
TYPE: Centaur & Arrighi.
In many copies, there is laid in loosely a 5½ x 8 slip of blue
Fabriano, on which is printed "The Gehenna Press sends along
with this broadside its hope for a healthy and peaceful New Year.
Northampton, 1969.", with pressmark XXV in red below.

1970
Printed from a woodcut by Wang Hui-Ming.
23¾ x 16. 1 sheet.
COLOPHON: "275 copies of Wang Hui-Ming's Fable of *A Toad and a
Crow* have been printed from the block at the Gehenna Press
February MCMLXX. 50 copies have been hand-colored by the
artist."
TYPE: Centaur; PAPER: Fabriano.

JOHN WOOLMAN'S DREAM OF THE FOX AND THE
CAT [in red]
With a woodcut drawn by LB & cut by John Keith.
26¼ x 23¾. 1 sheet, untrimmed. Printed in red & black.
COLOPHON: "JOHN WOOLMAN DESIGNED THIS DREAM
TO BE PLACED AT THE END OF HIS JOURNAL. TWO
YEARS AFTER HIS DEATH, THE QUAKER EDITORS
DELETED IT IN THE FIRST EDITION OF 1774. IT IS HERE
PRINTED FROM HIS MANUSCRIPT AT THE HISTORICAL

SOCIETY OF PENNSYLVANIA IN PHILADELPHIA. THE WOODCUT BY LEONARD BASKIN IS PRINTED FROM THE BLOCK. 500 COPIES OF THIS BROADSIDE, 50 OF WHICH ARE NUMBERED AND SIGNED, WERE STRUCK OFF AT THE GEHENNA PRESS, NORTHAMPTON, MASSACHUSETTS IN MARCH 1970." Copies 1–50 are signed by Keith & LB.
TYPE: Centaur & Arrighi; PAPER: Nideggen.

B17 · ON GETTING A NATURAL
On Getting a Natural ‖ · *For Gwendolyn Brooks* ·
A poem by Dudley Randall. With a drawing by LB, printed from a line cut.
25 x 10½. 1 sheet. Printed in red & black
COLOPHON: "500 copies printed at The Gehenna Press for The Broadside Press in July 1970; the portrait is by Leonard Baskin; 50 numbered copies have been signed by the poet and artist. ©Dudley Randall, 1970."
TYPE: Centaur & Arrighi.

CATALOGUE OF THE EXHIBITION
CURATED BY LISA UNGER BASKIN

The numbers in brackets refer to bibliography entries.

1 [1] · *On A Pyre of Withered Roses* · Poems by Leonard Baskin · New Haven · 1942
Collection of Pearl and Norman Rabinowitz.

2 [2] · *A Little Book of Natural History* · Engravings by Leonard Baskin · Worcester · 1951
Collection of David P. Becker.

3 [3] · *Some Engravings by Leonard Baskin* · Worcester · 1952
Collection of Lisa Unger Baskin.

4 [4] · *Castle Street Dogs* · Worcester · 1952
Collection of Lisa Unger Baskin.
  a. *Dogs.* Woodengraving block. 1¾ x 2¼.
  b. *Dogs.* Proof. 9⅛ x 6¼.
  c. *Dog.* Woodengraving block. 2 x 1⅞.
  d. *Dog.* Proof. 9⅛ x 6¼.
    Collection of Lisa Unger Baskin.

5 [5] · *The Tunning of Elynour Rummynge* · John Skelton · Worcester · 1953
Collection of Neil Elliott.
  a. Prospectus. 13 x 7.
    Collection of Gray Parrot and Christine John Covert.

6 [7] · *Blake and the Youthful Ancients* · Northampton · 1956
Collection of Neil Elliott.
  a. *George Richmond in his Engraving Costume.* Woodengraving block. 1¹¹⁄₁₆ x 1¹⁄₁₆.
    Collection of Lisa Unger Baskin.
  b. *George Richmond.* Proof. 5⅝ x 6⅝.*
  c. *Samuel Palmer.* Woodengraving block. 1½ x 1⅝.
    Collection of Lisa Unger Baskin.
  d. *Samuel Palmer.* Proof. 5⅝ x 6⅝.*
  e. Prospectus. Paste up for title page. 6¹⁵⁄₁₆ x 6.*
  f. Prospectus. 6¾ x 11½.*
  g. Leonard Baskin. Metcalf Printing. Photograph, 1956. 3½ x 5.*
  h. Romeo Cadieux and Baskin. Metcalf Printing. Photograph, 1956. 3½ x 5.*
    *Baskin Deposit. Beinecke Rare Book & Manuscript Library, Yale University.

7 [7] · *Thirteen Poems by Wilfred Owen* · Northampton · 1956
Collection of Estelle G. Unger.
  a. Pasteup. 13 x 9⅝.

b. Prospectus. 9½ x 12½.
Baskin Deposit. Beinecke Rare Book & Manuscript Library, Yale University.

8 [9] · *A Letter from Ernst Barlach* · Northampton · 1957
Collection of Liv Rockefeller and Kenneth Shure.

9 [10] · *Riddle Poems* · Emily Dickinson · Northampton · 1957
Collection of Liv Rockefeller and Kenneth Shure.

10 [11] · *Voyages* · *Six Poems from White Buildings* · Hart Crane · New York · 1957
Collection of Mata and Arthur Jaffee.
a. Title page design, pencil. 9⁷⁄₁₆ x 10⅞.
Baskin Deposit. Beinecke Rare Book & Manuscript Library, Yale University.

11 [14] · *Horned Beetles and Other Insects* · Northampton · 1958
Collection of Neil Elliott.
a. *Dynastes Hercules*. Etching plate. 3 x 8⅛.
Collection of Deborah and Philip Isaacson.
b. Prospectus. 9 x 6¼.
Collection of Gray Parrot and Christine John Covert.
c. Leonard Baskin with Etching Press, Northampton. Photograph, Steve Shapiro, 1963. 12⅝ x 8½.
Collection of Lisa Unger Baskin.

12 [15] · *The Seven Deadly Sins* · Poems by Anthony Hecht · Northampton · 1958
Collection of Lisa Unger Baskin.

13 [18] · *Homage To Redon* · Northampton · 1959
Collection of Ronald Cohen.

14 [20] · *Of Gardens* · Francis Bacon · Northampton · 1959
Collection of Ronald Cohen.

15 [21] · *Auguries of Innocence* · William Blake · Northampton · 1959
Collection of Liv Rockefeller and Kenneth Shure.
a. Prospectus. 3¾ x 10.
b. *Owl*. Preparatory drawing. 7 x 4⅜.
c. *Dog*. Preparatory drawing. 7 x 4⅜.
d. *Caterpillar*. Preparatory drawing. 7 x 4⅜.
e. *Inquisitor*. Preparatory drawing. 7 x 4⅜.
f. *Armoured Man*. Preparatory drawing. 7 x 4⅜.
g. *Armoured Man*. Woodengraving proof. 5¾ x 9¼.
Baskin Deposit, Beinecke Rare Book & Manuscript Library, Yale University.

h. *Owl*. Woodengraving block. Signed reverse "LB 1959". 5 x 3½.
   Collection of Lisa Unger Baskin.

16 [24] · *A Letter From Gustave Flaubert* · Northampton · 1960
   Collection of Pearl and Norman Rabinowitz.

17 [29] · *Four Portrait Busts by Francesco Laurana* · Northampton · 1960
   Collection of Janet and John Marqusee.
   a. *Ippolita Maria Sforza d'Aragona,* on Japan vellum. 9¾ x 14¼.
   b. Prospectus. 9¾ x 7¼.
      Collection of Lisa Unger Baskin.

18 [30] · *Of Garlands and Coronary* · Thomas Browne · Northampton · 1962
   Collection of Liv Rockefeller and Kenneth Shure.

19 [33] · *Encantadas* · Herman Melville · Northampton · 1963
   Collection of Mata and Arthur Jaffee.
   a. Woodcut block. 17 x 15.
      Collection of Lisa Unger Baskin.
   b. Woodcut proof. Rico Lebrun. 17 x 24½.
   c. Woodcut proof. Rico Lebrun. 22½ x 22.
      Collection of Hosea Baskin and Sarah Buttenwieser.
   d. Harold McGrath and Leonard Baskin, Clark Avenue. Photograph by Steve
      Shapiro, 1963. 13 x 8⅜.
      Collection of Lisa Unger Baskin.

20 [36] · *The Defense of Gracchus Babeuf* · Northampton · 1964
   The Bridwell Library, Southern Methodist University.

21 [37] · *A Letter from William Blake* · Northampton · 1964
   Collection of Estelle G. Unger.
   a. Prospectus. 14 x 6.
      Collection of Lisa Unger Baskin.

22 [38] · *A Human Document* · Robert A. Gardner · Northampton · 1964
   Collection of Liv Rockefeller and Kenneth Shure.
   a. Letter, typed, from Philip Hofer to Leonard Baskin. 14 February 1964. 8½ x 11.
      Baskin Deposit. Beinecke Rare Book & Manuscript Library, Yale University.

23 [42] · *Cancelleresca Bastarda Displayed* · Northampton · 1965
   Collection of Mata and Arthur Jaffee.
   a. Design for folio 8r. 6⁹⁄₁₆ x 10⅝.
   b. Pasteup for folio 8r, from dummy for book. 6¼ x 4⅞.

   c. Four progressive proofs for folio 8r. 6¼ x 10.

   d. Design for folio 3r. 6⁹⁄₁₆ x 10⅝.

   e. Design for prospectus. 5⅞ x 5¼ [folded].
     Baskin Deposit. Beinecke Rare Book & Manuscript Library, Yale University.

24 [48] · *A Checklist of the Publications of Thomas Bird Mosher of Portland Maine*
Northampton · 1966
Collection of David P. Becker.

25 [51] · *Flosculi Sententiarum* · Printers Flowers Moralised · Northampton · 1967
Collection of Janet and John Marqusee.

   a. Trial sheet "gold" with color indications. 9¼ x 4.

   b. Four sheets color trials for folio 25r. 15¼ x 9¼, 8 x 9¼.

   c. Folio 9r. 11 x 8.

   d. Manuscript of prospectus text, including a letter from Leonard Baskin to
     Lester Lloyd at Mackenzie and Harris, San Francisco. 11 x 16½.

   e. Prospectus. 11 x 8¼.
     Baskin Deposit. Beinecke Rare Book & Manuscript Library, Yale University.

26 [53] · *Aesopic* · Twenty Four Couplets by Anthony Hecht · Northampton · 1967
Collection of Mata and Arthur Jaffee.

   a. Letter, typed, from Anthony Hecht to Leonard Baskin. 26 January 1967. 8 x 11.

   b. Paste up. Annotated with a letter from Sidney Kaplan to Leonard Baskin,
     and Baskin's in return to Kaplan. 14 July 1967. 7⅞ x 8¼.
     Baskin Deposit. Beinecke Rare Book & Manuscript Library, Yale University.

27 [54] · *The Matchmaker's Lament* · Poems by Leonard Nathan · Northampton · 1967
Collection of Neil Elliott.

28 [57] · *Scholastic Dialogue* · Northampton · 1968
Collection of David P. Becker.

29 [60] · *The Selling of Joseph* · Samuel Sewall · Northampton · 1968
Collection of Lisa Unger Baskin.

30 [62] · *Hippolytos* · Euripides · Northampton · 1969
Special Collections, Carnegie Mellon University Libraries.

   a. Proof sheets with Robert Bagg's corrections. 15 x 9.
     Baskin Deposit. Beinecke Rare Book & Manuscript Library, Yale University.

   b. Prospectus. 12 x 8.
     Collection of Gray Parrot and Christine John Covert.

c. Leonard Baskin and Harold McGrath, Clarke Avenue. Photograph, c.1969. 5 x 6¾.
Collection of Lisa Unger Baskin.

31 [63] · *Laus Pictorum* · Northampton · 1969
Collection of Lucretia Baskin.

32 [66] · *West-Östlicher Divan* · J.W.V. Goethe · Northampton · 1970
Collection of Tobias Baskin and Laura Green.
   a. *Goethe.* Drawing, pen and ink. 7¾ x 4½.
   b. Drawing for page 132-3, pen and ink. 3¾ x 5½.
   Collection of Lisa Unger Baskin.

33 [67] · *Alcuin: A Dialogue* · Charles Brockden Brown · Northampton · 1970
Collection of Hosea Baskin and Sarah Buttenwieser.

34 [68] · *Tiresias* · Alfred Lord Tennyson · Northampton · 1970
Special Collections, University of Delaware Library.
   a. *Tiresias.* Block, engraved by John E. Benson. Signed "JEB · 68". 2¹³⁄₁₆ x 1¹³⁄₁₆.
   Collection of Hosea Baskin and Sarah Buttenwieser.

35 [69] · *Romeyn de Hooghe* · Northampton · 1971
Collection of Liv Rockefeller and Kenneth Shure.
   a. *R.* Drawing for title page. John E. Benson. 6 x 5¼.
   Collection of Lisa Unger Baskin.

36 [70] · *Anastatic Printing* · E.A. Poe · Northampton · 1970
Special Collections, Carnegie Mellon University Libraries.
   a. Title page. Trial proof. 8½ x 6.
   Collection of Emma and Sidney Kaplan.

37 [71] · *The Drawings of Jacob De Gheyn* · Northampton · 1972
Collection of Hosea Baskin and Sarah Buttenwieser.

38 [75] · *Othello* · William Shakespeare · Northampton · 1973
Collection of Lucretia Baskin.
   a. *Othello and Desdemona.* Drawing, pen and ink. 11¼ x 7¾.
   b. *Othello.* Drawing, pen and ink. 11½ x 7¾.
   Collection of Lisa Unger Baskin.

39 [76] · *The Coat Without a Seam* · *Sixty Poems 1930-1972* · Stanley Kunitz
Northampton · 1974
Collection of Tobias Baskin and Laura Green.

a. Kunitz and Baskin at Fort Hill c.1973. Photograph by Peter Farb. 8 x 10.
    Collection of Lisa Unger Baskin.

40 [78] · *Some Considerations on the Keeping of Negroes* · John Woolman · Northampton · 1975
    Collection of Emma and Sidney Kaplan.
    a. Title page preparatory design, pencil. 8½ x 5½.
    b. Title page proof. 8 x 6.
    c. Title page proof. 8 x 6.
        Baskin Deposit. Beinecke Rare Book & Manuscript Library. Yale University.

41 [80] · *A Primer of Birds* · Ted Hughes · Lurley, Devon · 1981
    The Bridwell Library, Southern Methodist University.
    a. Manuscript. List of poems with preliminary designs for title page. 9⅛ x 7⅛.
    b. Drawing of title page, dummy. 10¾ x 5¾.
    c. Pasteup of title page. 10⅝ x 5¾.
    d. *Hanging Bird*. Preparatory drawing. 10⅝ x 11½.
    e. *Hanging Bird*. Woodcut, 1st state. First impression. April 1981. 9½ x 5¼.
    f. *Monkey Eating Eagle*. Woodcut, proof. 10¼ x 5¾.
    g. *Standing Bird*. Woodcut, proof. 10¼ x 5¾.
    h. *Dead Crow*. Woodcut, proof. 10¼ x 5¾.
    i. *Phoenix*. Woodcut, trial proof. 10¾ x 5¾.
    j. *Sparrow*. Ted Hughes. Manuscript. 9⅞ x 7¼.
    k. *Two Marabou Storks*. Ted Hughes. Manuscript. 9⅞ x 7¼.
    l. *Sparrow*. Galley proofs, corrections by Ted Hughes and Leonard Baskin. 24 x 8½.
    m. Printing Office, Lurley, Bruce Chandler. 1981. Photograph 5 x 7.
    n. Printing Office, Lurley, Robert Wakefield. 1981. Photograph 5 x 7.
    o. Printing Office, Lurley, Baskin. Wakefield and Chandler. 1981. Photograph 5 x 7.
        Collection of Lisa Unger Baskin.

42 [81] · *A Gehenna Alphabet* · Lurley, Devon · 1982
    Collection of Emma and Sidney Kaplan.
    a. Letter, manuscript, Sidney Kaplan to Leonard Baskin, 1 November 1981. 8 x 11.
    b. *H*. Drawing, pen and ink. 7⅝ x 5½.
    c. Typographic arrangement for *H*. 8½ x 11.
        Collection of Lisa Unger Baskin.

43 [82] · *Diptera · A Book of Flies & Other Insects* · Lurley, Devon · 1983
    The Bridwell Library, Southern Methodist University.
    Cave Cricket. Etching, progressive proofs.
    a. 1st state, touched with ink. 9¼ x 6.
    b. 1st state. 12 October 1982. 9¼ x 6.

c. 1st state, touched with watercolor. 13 October 1982. 9¼ x 6.

d. 2nd state. 13 October 1982. 9¼ x 6.

e. 3rd state. 15 October 1982. 9¼ x 6.

f. 4th state. 20 October 1982. 9¼ x 6.

g. Printer's color trial. 9¼ x 6.

h. Counterproof of color trial. 9¼ x 6.

Cockroach. Etching, preparatory material.

i. Etching plate. 1¾ x 4.

j. 1st state, four color and paper trials. 10⅜ x 15½.

k. 2nd state, four color and paper trials. 12 and 14 November 1982. 10¼ x 15¼.

l. Two color trials. 7 January 1983. 10¼ x 7¼.

m. Touched proof. 9⅞ x 10¼.

n. *Dragon Fly*. Etching, color trial. 7 x 8½.

o. Page proof. 31 March 1983. 11½ x 7¾.

Collection of Lisa Unger Baskin.

44 [83] · *Unknown Dutch Artists* · Lurley, Devon · 1983

Collection of Hosea Baskin and Sarah Buttenwieser.

a. Title page, press proof. 11 x 7½.

Gillen R. Lelijkerd. Preparatory material.

b. Watercolor and page design manuscript. 10¼ x 7¾.

c. Corrected proof. 10¼ x 7¾.

d. Etching, color proof with notes. 16 January 1983. 6¼ x 10.

J. van Cipier. Preparatory material.

e. Double page with manuscript, etching proofs and corrected proof. 11½ x 15¾.

f. Etching, color proof. 11½ x 7¼.

Collection of Lisa Unger Baskin.

45 [84] · *Mokomaki* · Leeds · 1985

Collection of Lucretia Baskin.

a. Title page, paste up. 12¼ x 9¼.

b. Title page. 14½ x 7⅝.

c. Etching proof. 14½ x 9¼.

Collection of Lisa Unger Baskin.

46 [85] · *Hermaika* · Leeds · 1986

Collection of Tobias Baskin and Laura Green.

47 [86] · *Icones Librorum Artifices* · Leeds · 1988

The Bridwell Library, Southern Methodist University.

a. Manuscript list of engravers, etc. 9 1/2 x 7.
b. Manuscript list of engravers, etc. 8 x 9.
c. Design for title page, ink. 14 3/4 x 8 1/4.
d. Design for title page, ink. 12 3/4 x 9 1/2.
e. Design for title page, pencil. 12 1/2 x 9 7/8.
f. Design for title page, ink. 12 1/2 x 8 3/4.
g. Title page, proof, paste up. 15 3/4 x 11 1/4.
h. Manuscript draft of letter, Leonard Baskin to Robert Wakefield. 7 June 1987. 2 pgs. 10 x 6 1/4.
i. Letter, Robert Wakefield to Leonard Baskin. n.d. 11 1/2 x 8 1/4.

Etienne Delaune. Preparatory material.
j. Manuscript of text. 4 1/4 x 4 3/4.
k. Manuscript of text. 6 7/8 x 9 1/2.
l. Page design, watercolor. 12 1/2 x 12 1/2.
m. Design trial. 12 1/4 x 6 1/4.
n. Layout, drawing with text. 11 3/4 x 6 1/4.
o. Layout, etching proof with manuscript. 12 1/2 x 12 1/2.
p. Corrected page proof. 13 3/4 x 9 3/4.
q. Etching proof, 1st state. 7 1/2 x 5 1/2.
r. Etching proof, 2nd state. 5 1/2 x 5.

Anne Allen. Preparatory material.
s. Manuscript of text. 9 1/2 x 7.
t. Manuscript. 22 July 1987. 9 1/2 x 7.
u. Manuscript. 1 June 1987. 9 1/2 x 7.
v. First drawing design, watercolor and pencil. 12 1/2 x 12 1/2.
w. Manuscript with design and text. 8 1/2 x 5 1/2.
x. Manuscript of text. 10 1/2 x 7 1/4.
y. Page design, manuscript. 12 1/2 x 12 1/2.
z. Page proof. 14 3/4 x 9 3/4.
aa. Sheet with etching proofs, color trials. 12 1/2 x 9 3/4.

Maria Sibylla Merian. Preparatory material.
bb. Manuscript of text. 23 July 1987. 9 1/2 x 6 7/8.
cc. Watercolor drawing, page design. 12 1/2 x 12 1/2.
dd. Page proof with corrections. 12 1/2 x 8 5/8.
ee. Page proof with portrait. 15 1/2 x 11 1/4.
ff. Etching, 1st state, touched proof. 12 1/2 x 10.
gg. Etching proofs, 1st state, color trials. 2 August 1987. 12 1/2 x 10.

Thomas Anselm. Preparatory material.
hh. Page design with etching proof, manuscript. 12 1/2 x 9 1/4.

ii. Etching proof with corrections. 15½ x 10¼.
Collection of Lisa Unger Baskin.

48 [87] · *Twelve Sculptors* · Leeds · 1988
The John Hay Library, Brown University.
a. *William Rimmer.* Touched monotype. 10⅞ x 8.
b. *Frederic Macmonnies.* Monotype. 10⅞ x 8.
Collection of Tobias Baskin and Laura Green.

49 [91] · *Irises · A Book of Etchings* · Leeds · 1988
Special Collections, University of Delaware Library.
a. *Iris.* Etching, color trial, touched. 12⅜ x 12½.
b. *Iris.* Etching, proof on blue paper. 6¾ x 5.
c. *Iris.* Etching, 1st state, touched. 1987. 12½ x 12½.
d. *Iris.* Etching, 2nd state, paper trial. 12½ x 12½.
e. *Iris.* Etching, 3rd state, color trial. 12½ x 12½.
Collection of Lisa Unger Baskin.

50 [92] · *Fancies Bizarreries & Ornamented Grotesques* · Leeds · 1989
Collection of Mata and Arthur Jaffee.
a. Title page, first trial. 9½ x 6¾.
b. Title page, second trial. 9½ x 6¼.
c. Title page, third trial. 9½ x 6¼.
d. Title page, fourth trial. 9¾ x 6½.
Dragonfly. Preparatory material.
e. Pencil drawing. 10 x 7.
f. Etching, 1st state. 10 x 7.
g. Etching, 1st state, color trial. 10 x 7.
h. Etching, 2nd state, 1 January 1989. 10 x 7.
i. Etching, final proof, printed by R. Wakefield. 10 x 7.
Grotesque with Thistle. Preparatory material.
j. Preparatory drawing, ink. 10 x 6½.
k. Preparatory drawing, pencil. 10 x 6½.
l. Etching, 1st state, touched. 10 x 6½.
m. Etching, 2nd state. 10 x 6½.
n. Etching, 2nd state, color trial. 10 x 6½.
Collection of Lisa Unger Baskin.

51 [93] · *Gypsy & Other Poems* · James Baldwin · Leeds · 1989
Collection of Lucretia Baskin.
a. Design for title page. 11¾ x 8¾.

b. Title page. 12 x 9.
c. *JB 1955*. Pencil drawing. 11¾ x 9.
d. *JB 1955*. Etching proof. 11½ x 9.
e. *James Baldwin*. Drawing, pen and ink. 11¾ x 8¾.
f. *James Baldwin*. Nine etching trials. 15½ x 11½.
g. *James Baldwin*. Four etching proofs. 21½ x 17½.
   Collection of Lisa Unger Baskin.

52 [95] · *Capriccio* · Poems by Ted Hughes · Leeds · 1990
Special Collections, Carnegie Mellon University Libraries and
Special Collections, University of Delaware Library.
a. Letter, manuscript. Ted Hughes to Leonard and Lisa Baskin, 21 October
   1989. 8 x 10.
b. Title page, drawing. 19 x 12¾.
c. Title page, woodcut, 1st state, trial proof. 15¼ x 11.
d. Title page, woodcut, 2nd state, pasteup. 15½ x 11.
e. *Descent*. Preparatory drawing, pen and ink. 9 x 12.
f. *Fanaticism*. Etching, 1st state, touched. March 1990. 14 x 10¼.
g. *Fanaticism*. Etching, 2nd state, color trial. March 1990. 14 x 10¼.
h. *Possession*. Woodcut, proof. 20¾ x 14½.
i. *Mythographers*. Etching, color trial. 6½ x 11¾.
The Error. Woodcut, preparatory material.
j. Preparatory drawing, pencil. 1989. 15¾ x 11.
k. Woodcut block. 16 x 10¼.
l. Woodcut, 1st state. 17¾ x 12.
m. Woodcut, touched proof. 18 x 10¾.
n. Woodcut proof. 20 x 14¼.
o. *Rules of the Game*. Preparatory pencil drawing, etchings, 1st and 2nd states,
   six trial proofs. 21½ x 16½.
p. *Familiar*. Etching proof. 6¼ x 11½.
Chlorophyll. Etching, progressive proofs.
q. 1st state. 10 x 12½.
r. 2nd state, color trial. 12 x 13½.
s. 3rd state. 11 x 14.
t. 4th state. 10 x 13½.
u. 5th state. 13 x 12.
v. Prospectus. 22 x 12½.
   Collection of Lisa Unger Baskin.

53 [96] · *Sibyls* · Poems by Ruth Fainlight · Leeds · 1991
Collection of Kenneth and Peter Schrager.
   a. *Profiles*. Woodcut proof. 19½ x 14½.
   b. *Profiles*. Woodcut, touched proof. 14 x 12.
   c. *The Egg Mother*. Woodcut, color trial. 19 x 12½.
   d. *Elegant Sibyl*. Woodcut proof. 21½ x 14½.
   e. *Facts About the Sibyl*. Woodcut, touched proof with printing notations. 17 x 14.
   f. *Inward*. Preparatory drawing, watercolor. 7⅛ x 7½.
   g. Colophon. Woodcut proof. 12 x 10½.
   h. Prospectus. 25 x 12½.
      Collection of Lisa Unger Baskin.

54 [97] · *Grotesques* · Leeds · 1991
Collection of Lucretia Baskin.
   a. Etching for marginalia. Three trials, one touched. 11½ x 9¼.
   b. Etching for marginalia. Three color trials and page design. 11½ x 9½.
   c. *Spike-necked Bird*. Preparatory drawing, ink. 12¾ x 9½.
   d. *Spike-necked Bird*. Etching, color trial. 11½ x 9½.
   e. *Punch Riding A Bird*. Preparatory drawing, ink. 8 June 1990. L.A. 11½ x 9½.
   f. *Punch Riding A Bird*. Etching, color trial. 11½ x 9½.
   g. *Punch Riding A Bird*. Etching, maculatura. 11½ x 9½.
   h. *Swelled Ornament*. Preparatory drawings, ink. Virginia, 1990, 8 January 1991. 11½ x 9½.
   i. *Swelled Ornament*. Etching, color trial. 13¾ x 10¼.
   j. *Running Imp*. Three preparatory drawings, ink. 31 August 1990. 13½ x 10½.
   k. *Running Imp*. Etching, color trial and proof. 28 December, 1990. 11¼ x 9¼.
   l. *Running Imp*. Etching, color trial proofs. 11½ x 9¼.
   m. *Arabesque*. Etching, color trial. 8¼ x 11½.
   n. *New Dragonfly*. Preparatory drawing, ink. 12½ x 19.
   o. *New Dragonfly*. Etching, 1st state, proof. 23 November 1990. 10¼ x 10½.
   p. *New Dragonfly*. Etching, color trial proof. 11½ x 9½.
   q. Prospectus. 8 x 7¼.
      Collection of Lisa Unger Baskin.
   r. Printing Office, Leeds. Michael Kuch. Photograph by Noel Chanan. November, 1991. 12 x 16.
      Collection of Michael Kuch.
   s. Leonard Baskin, Printing Office, Leeds. Photograph by Noel Chanan. November 1991. 8 x 10.

55 [B1] · *The Gehenna Press* · Worcester · 1952
Collection of Hosea Baskin and Sarah Buttenwieser.
    a. Vandercook proof press, 'D' platen. 19th century. Photograph c.1952. 2⅝ x 2½.
       Collection of Lisa Unger Baskin.

56 [B2] · *Jack Plain Dealing* · Worcester · 1952
Smith College Library, Rare Book Room.

57 [B3] · *Easter 1916* · William Butler Yeats · Worcester · 1952
Smith College Library, Rare Book Room.
    a. Prospectus. 6⅝ x 11¼.
    b. Preparatory drawing, on reverse of prosectus, pencil. 6⅝ x 11¼.
       Collection of Lisa Unger Baskin.

58 [B4] · *A Candle* · Sir John Suckling · 1952
Collection of Tobias Baskin and Laura Green.

59 [B5] · *A Poem, As Consequent, Etc.* · Walt Whitman · Northampton · 1955
Collection of Emma and Sidney Kaplan.

60 [B6] · *Pike* · A Poem by Ted Hughes · Northampton · 1959
Collection of David P. Becker.
    a. Gehenna Press Catalogue, 1959, announcing *Pike*. 9 x 12.
       Collection of Lisa Unger Baskin.

61 [B8] · *On The Nature of Inspiration* · William Morris · Northampton · 1962
Collection of Lisa Unger Baskin.

62 [B9] · *William Blake from Jerusalem* · Northampton · 1964
Collection of Lisa Unger Baskin.

63 [B11] · *The Eemis Stane* · Hugh MacDiarmid · Northampton · 1967
Collection of Emma and Sidney Kaplan.
    a. Prospectus. 4⅞ x 7.
       Collection of Lisa Unger Baskin.

64 [B14] · *Melville on Piranesi* · Northampton · 1969
Collection of Lisa Unger Baskin.

65 [B16] · *John Woolman's Dream of the Fox and the Cat* · Northampton · 1970
Collection of Emma and Sidney Kaplan.

66 · Assorted ephemera.

67 · Shop Sign for The Gehenna Press. Cut and gilded slate. John E. Benson. circa 1965.
Lent by The Gehenna Press.

PLATES

ON A PYRE OF WITHERED ROSES

poems by

LEONARD BASKIN

the gehenna press
mcmxlii

ɪ · On A Pyre of Withered Roses · 1942 · [ɪ]

A LITTLE BOOK
OF NATURAL HISTORY
ENGRAVINGS ⟨ ⟩ BY
LEONARD   BASKIN

THE GEHENNA PRESS
WORCESTER
1951

3 · Some Engravings by Leonard Baskin · 1952 · [3]

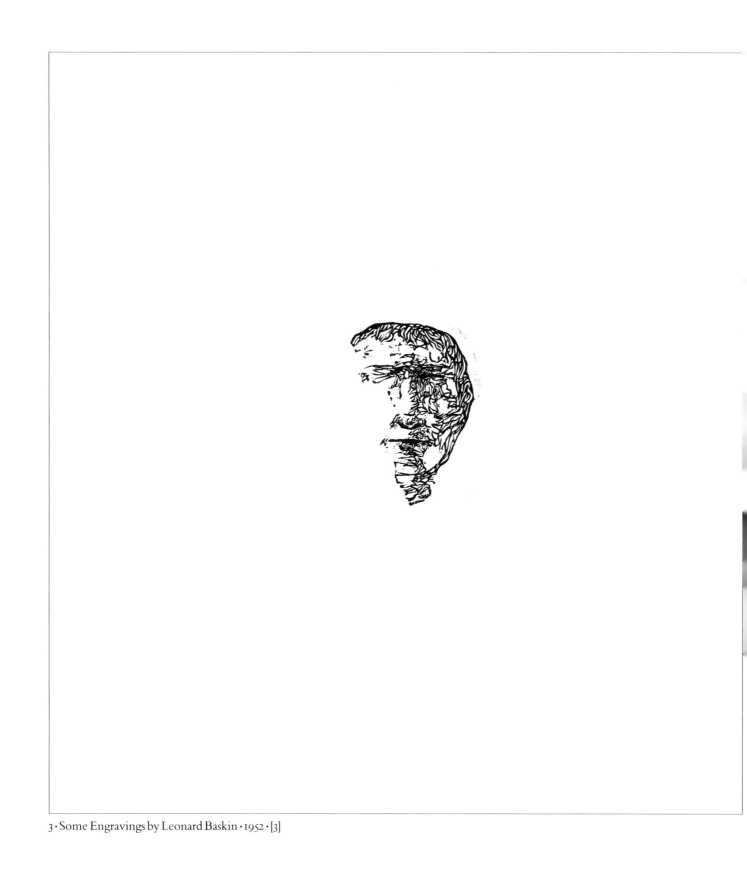

3 · Some Engravings by Leonard Baskin · 1952 · [3]

castle
street
dogs

Wood Engravings by Leonard Baskin

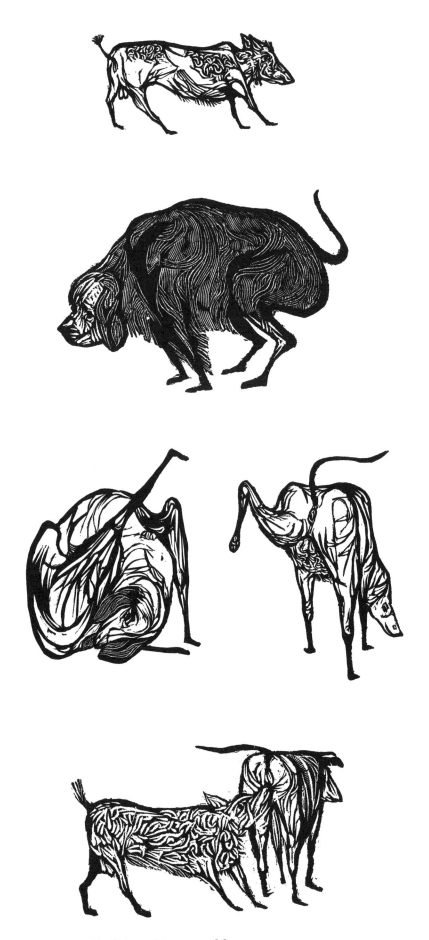

4 · Castle Street Dogs · 1952 · [4]

20 copies of CASTLE STREET DOGS have been printed by E. and L. Baskin at the Gehenna Press on Castle St. in Worcester Massachusetts.　August 1952

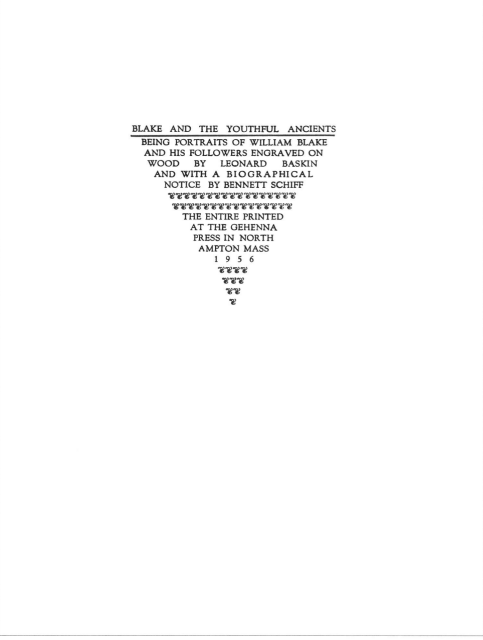

BLAKE AND THE YOUTHFUL ANCIENTS
BEING PORTRAITS OF WILLIAM BLAKE
AND HIS FOLLOWERS ENGRAVED ON
WOOD BY LEONARD BASKIN
AND WITH A BIOGRAPHICAL
NOTICE BY BENNETT SCHIFF
THE ENTIRE PRINTED
AT THE GEHENNA
PRESS IN NORTH
AMPTON MASS
1 9 5 6

6 · Blake and the Youthful Ancients · 1956 · [7]

POEMS
WILFRED OWEN

"You are not an artist, you are an actor. You pretend to have feelings, but I create visions and feelings, moods and sensations, by direct transmission, without a medium, like the telegraph."

That's all right, if feelings could be invoked by order. Blue means this, yellow means that; perhaps it does, but whether it has the heavenly power to turn the Ought to Must is the question. When colors and lines form human figures—or even vice versa—they have this power, for they get it from the human soul. It often happens that colors and shapes seen on walls or other things suddenly turn into pictures when a soul is given them through fantasy or imagination; by this act they are drawn into my

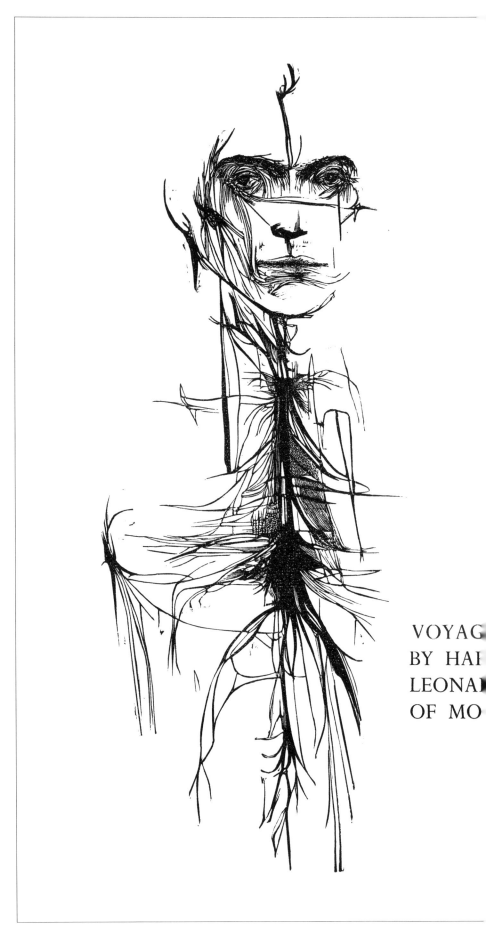

VOYAG
BY HAI
LEONA
OF MO

10 · Voyages · 1957 · [11]

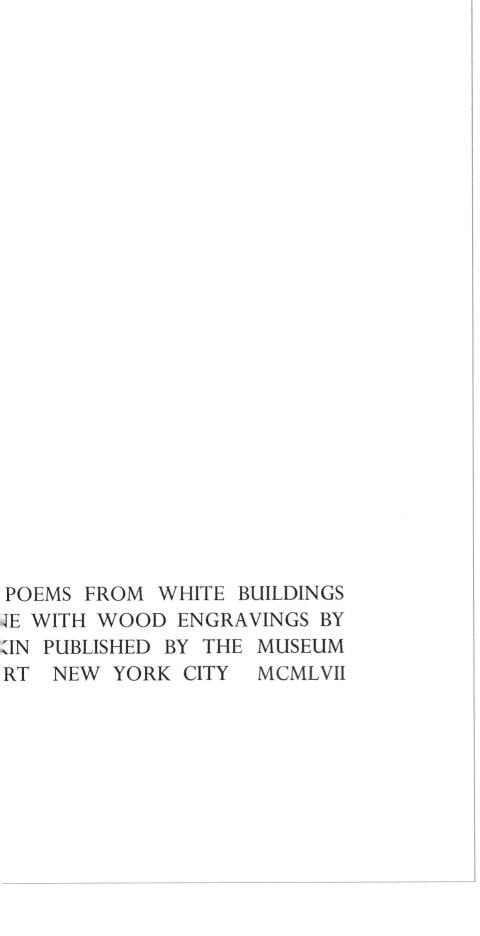

POEMS FROM WHITE BUILDINGS
　E WITH WOOD ENGRAVINGS BY
　IN PUBLISHED BY THE MUSEUM
　RT　NEW YORK CITY　MCMLVII

11 · Horned Beetles and Other Insects · 1958 · [14]

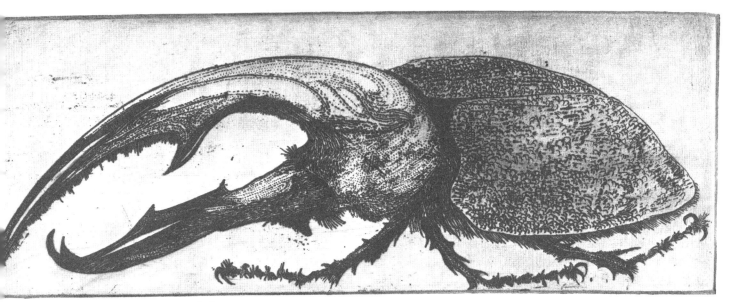

Horned Beetles and Other Insects · 1958 · [14]

11 · Horned Beetles and Other Insects · 1958 · [14]

WRATH

I saw in stalls of pearl the heavenly hosts,
Gentle as down, and without private parts.
"Dies Irae," they sang, and I could smell
The dead-white phosphorus of sacred hearts.

AUGURIES OF INNOCENCE
BY
WILLIAM BLAKE

WOOD ENGRAVINGS
BY
LEONARD BASKIN

PRINTED
FOR
THE PRINT CLUB
OF
PHILADELPHIA

AT THE
GEHENNA PRESS
1959

AUGURIES OF INNOCENCE

To see a World in a Grain of Sand
And a Heaven in a Wild Flower,
Hold Infinity in the palm of your hand
And Eternity in an hour.
A Robin Red breast in a Cage
Puts all Heaven in a Rage.
A dove house fill'd with doves & Pigeons
Shudders Hell thro' all its regions.

A dog starv'd at his Master's Gate
Predicts the ruin of the State.
A Horse misus'd upon the Road
Calls to Heaven for Human blood.
Each outcry of the hunted Hare
A fibre from the Brain does tear.
A Skylark wounded in the wing,
A Cherubim does cease to sing.
The Game Cock clip'd & arm'd for fight
Does the Rising Sun affright.
Every Wolf's & Lion's howl
Raises from Hell a Human Soul.
The wild deer, wand'ring here & there,
Keeps the Human Soul from Care.
The Lamb misus'd breeds Public strife
And yet forgives the Butcher's Knife.
The Bat that flits at close of Eve
Has left the Brain that won't Believe.

The Owl that calls upon the Night
Speaks the Unbeliever's fright.

Nought can deform the Human Race
Like to the Armour's iron brace.

15 · Auguries of Innocence · 1959 · [21]

When Gold & Gems adorn the Plow
To peaceful Arts shall Envy Bow.
A Riddle or the Cricket's Cry
Is to Doubt a fit Reply.
The Emmet's Inch & Eagle's Mile
Make Lame Philosophy to smile.
He who Doubts from what he sees
Will ne'er Believe, do what you Please.
If the Sun & Moon should doubt,
They'd immediately Go out.
To be in a Passion you Good may do,
But no Good if a Passion is in you.
The Whore & Gambler, by the State
Licenc'd, build that Nation's Fate.
The Harlot's cry from Street to Street
Shall weave Old England's winding Sheet.
The Winner's Shout, the Loser's Curse,
Dance before dead England's Hearse.
Every Night & every Morn
Some to Misery are Born.
Every Morn & every Night
Some are Born to sweet delight.
Some are Born to sweet delight,
Some are Born to Endless Night.
We are led to Believe a Lie
When we see not Thro' the Eye
Which was Born in a Night to perish in a Night
When the Soul Slept in Beams of Light.
God Appears & God is Light
To those poor Souls who dwell in Night,
But does a Human Form Display
To those who Dwell in Realms of day.

place in the annals of Italian art. Enthusiasm for his rare productions is now wide-spread among connoisseurs and practising artists. He has even achieved the eminence of a number of forgeries. ❦ Some of Laurana's latter-day fame can be related to the fabulous resurgence of Piero della Francesca as a painter dear to the twentieth century. Piero, too, was practically forgotten in the intervening years. Montaigne, who reluctantly spent a night in Borgo S. Sepolcro in 1580, wrote in his journal, "There is nothing of artistic interest here," when all he need have done was to step into the Municipio to see the *Resurrection*. But, since the '20s of this century, the abstract properties and geometric organization of Piero's paintings have seemed so much in accord with modern critical criteria and with modern art itself that Piero has outstripped his contemporaries in present-day esteem. Laurana's brief approach to Piero's orbit, his highly original handling of technical and representational problems, his variability of style, his preference for the subjective and the irrational rather than the objective and the rational—even his secretiveness have all combined to rescue Laurana's private language from the limbo of the dead tongues. His art is legible to us today and awakens in us the joy of recognition.

❦ ❦ ❦

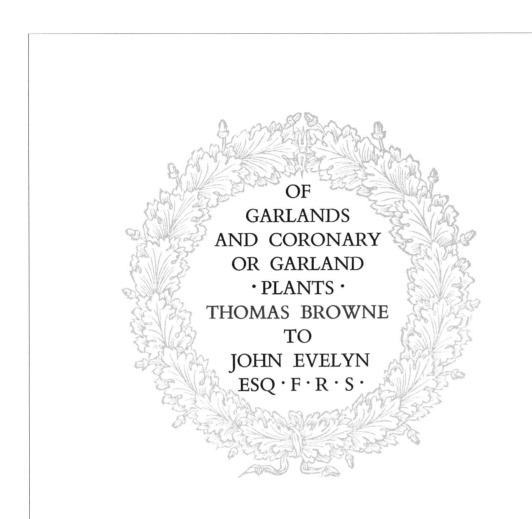

OF
GARLANDS
AND CORONARY
OR GARLAND
· PLANTS ·
THOMAS BROWNE
TO
JOHN EVELYN
ESQ · F · R · S ·

ENCANTADAS

TWO SKETCHES

FROM

HERMAN MELVILLE'S

ENCHANTED

ISLES

WITH WOODCUTS

BY

RICO LEBRUN

PRINTED

AT

THE GEHENNA PRESS

IN

NORTHAMPTON

MCMLXIII

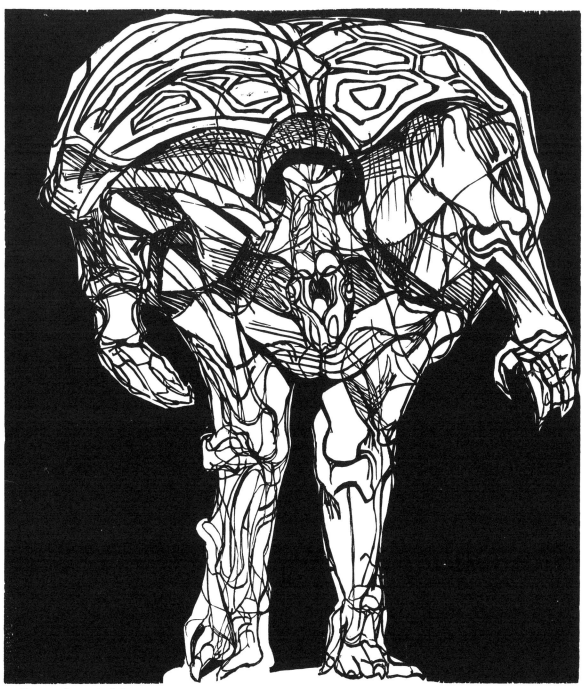

19 · Encantadas · 1963 · [33]

THE DEFENSE OF GRACCHUS BABEUF
BEFORE THE HIGH COURT OF VENDOME

EDITED & TRANSLATED

WITH AN ESSAY

ON BABEUF

BY

JOHN ANTHONY SCOTT

WITH

TWENTY-ONE

ETCHED PORTRAITS

BY

THOMAS CORNELL

THE GEHENNA PRESS

NORTHAMPTON

1964

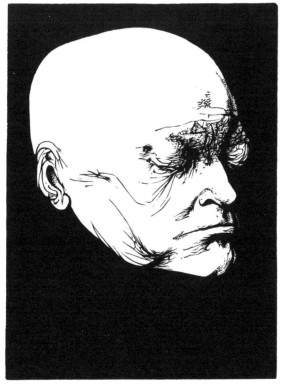

21 · A Letter From William Blake · 1964 · [37]

Nous avons tous assez de force pours supporter les maux d'autrui

ABCDEF
GHIJKL
MNOPQR
STUVWX
YZ

23 · Cancelleresca Bastarda Displayed · 1965 · [42]

Dios Me Libre De Hombre De Un Libro

A B C D

E F G

H I J K L M

N O P

Q R S T U V

W

X Y Z

23 · Cancelleresca Bastarda Displayed · 1965 · [42]

LA FAME NON VUOL LEGGI

23 · Cancelleresca Bastarda Displayed · 1965 · [42]

205

25 · Flosculi Sententiarum · 1967 · [51]

25 · Flosculi Sententiarum · 1967 · [51]

ÆSOPIC

TWENTY FOUR COUPLETS BY ANTHONY HECHT TO ACCOMPANY
THE THOMAS BEWICK WOOD ENGRAVINGS FOR · SELECT FABLES ·
WITH AN AFTERWORD ON THE BLOCKS BY PHILIP HOFER

AT THE GEHENNA PRESS IN NORTHAMPTON · MASSACHUSETTS

26 · Aesopic · 1967 · [53]

The Thief and the Dog

Hell, too, hath mansions, where none need provide
A sop for Cerberus to get inside.

THE MATCHMAKER'S BUSINESS ADDRESS

I've got this sign, reads "OUT"; I hang it up
When one too many lonelies gets me down;
She beats the door, she swears, then goes away;
I pity her, but dream I'm out of town—
One bench I dream, reserved by Florida;
It has a name—Retirement—and will drift
In peace for on and on, with plenty room
If any single mermaid needs a lift.
Now here's this office chair I've trained to cry;
"Hey, Yukel, please remember! It's New York."
I do and turn the sign around to read
I'm ready for reality or work.
Later, I'll miss a bus, run blocks, and sweat
Up stairs to soothe the hare-lip that your pity
Singles out but cannot cure or love;
What bachelor among you sees her soul is pretty?
Each knock pains like a punch. She knows I'm in
To ask that final question: What, my dear,
Is left when the lucky ones pair off and go,
And you back off, rejected by the mirror?
A deal! I'll send my bench to Israel;
And you, your excess hope; we'll start with need;
We'll tear this town apart until we learn
What charity is left after our greed.

27 · The Matchmakers Lament · 1967 · [54]

THE MATCHMAKER AT SEA

You'd think I was Spinoza standing here
And studying this wrinkled swatch of green
That goes for on and on. Inside, I too
Cut cards, guzzled, fingered a magazine,
But kept on feeling under foot the roll
Of dark wet tons in which the biggest fish
Was dumbness wrapped in cold. You have to drown
Your mind to think such lovers have no wish
To talk of love, or share a single thing
Except (I've read) the eggs and sperm they drop
Outside of them on neutral ground. It must be
All that pressure on them from the top,
Like conscience. Yet they eat each other too,
So it's no better giving up the speech
Of love or hate. Or maybe it's cold blood,
I'd rather be Columbus out to reach
A hopeless place of riches lost by men
And women speaking any tongue, not mine,
But human, one at least I half could learn
Or maybe learn some little friendly sign
For hunger and its thanks—Spinoza, no.
Standing on a chip of rolling wood,
That swims eternity, to find a law
In all this coldness may be one man's good;
But I am made for other, lesser ends:
I need a friend, I need a dozen friends.

Culs de Lampe · 1968 · [56] · *not exhibited*

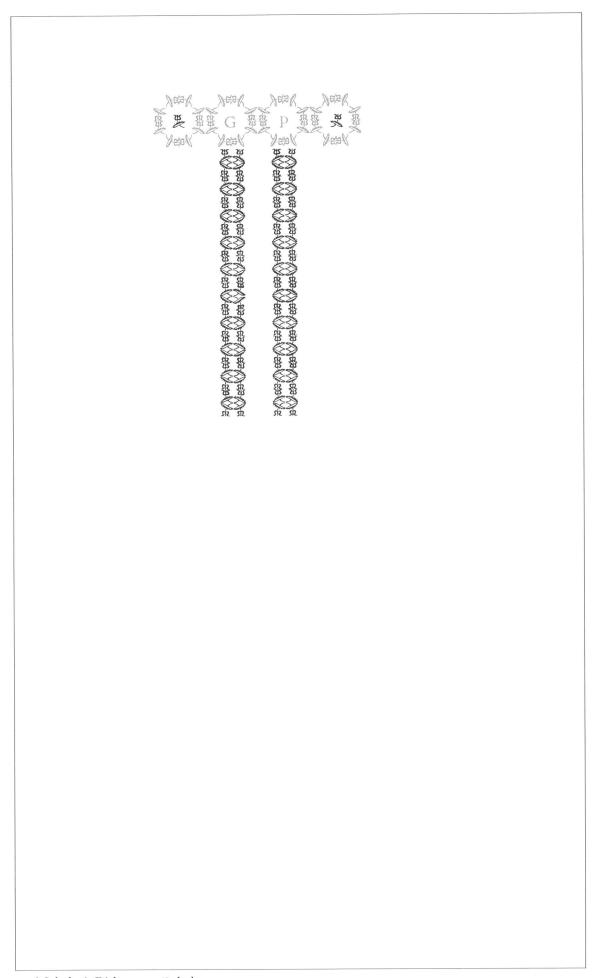

PIPPIN What is a letter?

ALCUIN The guardian of history.

PIPPIN What is a word?

ALCUIN The expositor of the mind.

P. What produces a word?

A. The tongue.

P. What is the tongue?

A. The whip of the air.

P. What is the air?

A. The guardian of life.

P. What is life?

A. The joy of the blessed, the sorrow of the miserable,
   the expectation of death.

P. What is death?

A. The inevitable issue, an uncertain pilgrimage,
   the tears of the living, the thief of man.

P. What is man?

A. The possession of death, a transient wayfarer, a guest.

P. How is man situated?

A. Like a lantern in the wind.

P. Where is he placed?

A. Between six walls.

P. Which?

A. Above, below, in front, back, on the right and the left.

P. How many companions has he?

A. Four.

P. Who are they?

A. Heat, cold, dryness, moisture.

P. In how many ways is he variable?

A. In six.

P. What are they?

A. Hunger and satiety; rest and toil; wakefulness and sleep.

P. What is sleep?

A. The image of death.

Printed in an edition of 25 copies at The Gehenna Press
Northampton, Massachusetts
June, 1968

The
method
of teaching
by means of
question and answer
was prevalent in the medieval cathedral schools; this form
of catechism was an outgrowth of
the Socratic Method handed down
through the writings of Plato.

.   .   .   .

This dialogue is from *Disputatio Regalis et Nobilissimi
Iuvenis Pippini cum Albino Scholastico* Alcuin: 8th century.
Alcuin (Albinus) was the tutor of Pippin, son of Charlemagne.

∵ SAMUEL SEWALL ∵
∵

THE SELLING OF JOSEPH

A MEMORIAL

THE GEHENNA PRESS
MCMLXVIII

there be made of that Celebrated Warning,

Caveat Emptor!

And all things considered, it would conduce more to the Welfare of the Province, to have White Servants for a Term of Years, than to have Slaves for Life. Few can endure to hear of a Negro's being made free; and indeed they can seldom use their freedom well; yet their continual aspiring after their forbidden Liberty, renders them Unwilling Servants. And there is such a disparity in their Conditions, Colour & Hair, that they can never embody with us, and grow up into orderly Families, to the Peopling of the Land: but still remain in our Body Politick as a kind of extravasat Blood. As many Negro men as there are among us, so many empty places there are in our Train Bands, and the places taken up of Men that might make Husbands for our Daughters. And the Sons and Daughters of *New England*

8

BRESDIN TO REDON
six letters 1870 to 1881
edited by Roseline Bacou
translated by Seymour S Weiner
The Gehenna Press
1969

Aphrodite THE POWER I POSSESS IS SEX,
PASSION, LOVE, WHICH
YOU HUMANS, IN HONORING
ME, CELEBRATE IN
YOUR DIVERSE WAYS.
I'm no less the darling of heaven.
I am the goddess Aphrodite.
My subjects live in the Mediterranean sunlight
From the Black Sea to the Atlantic beaches
And those responsive to my sacred privileges,
My whims, my implacable caresses, I reward;
I delight them; but I stir up trouble
For any who ignore me, or belittle me,
And who do it out of stubborn pride.
Does it surprise you that gods are passionate,
That they like humans to honor them?
If you will listen to this story
The truth of my words is quickly proven.
There lives in this province of Trozen
Hippolytos, the illegitimate child
Of Theseus and his Amazon mistress.
The old king of this province,
Pittheus, made him his protegé.
Now this young man, alone
Among his contemporaries,
Says freely I am a despicable goddess.
Marriage is anathema to him,
He goes to bed with no girl.
The goddess he adores is Artemis, a virgin,
Apollo's sister, the daughter of Zeus.
Our young friend thinks *her*
Kind of divinity the most exhilarating.
In the pale green forest they are inseparable,
They drive their killer hounds until the wildlife,
Squirrels as well as stags, is extinct.

12

Woher ich kam? Es ist noch eine Frage,
Mein Weg hierher, der ist mir kaum bewußt,
Heut nun und hier am himmelfrohen Tage
Begegnen sich, wie Freunde, Schmerz und
   Lust.
O süßes Glück, wenn beide sich vereinen!
Einsam, wer möchte lachen, möchte weinen?

132

32 · West-Östlicher Divan· 1970 · [66]

12

My route? It hardly comes to mind.
But here and now this sky-filled day
A meeting between grief and joy
Like old, old friends.
O sweetest fortune could they unify—
Disjoined, who cares to laugh, who
                        cares to cry?

133

ALFRED LORD TENNYSON

34 · Tiresias · 1970 · [68]

ROMEYN DE HOOGHE
TO THE BURGERMASTERS OF HAARLEM

35 · Romeyn de Hooghe to the Burgermasters of Haarlem · 1971 · [69]

large paintings can be executed there. 13. A garden where the students will be able to practice the drawing of flower gardens (parterres), flowers, paths, trees. 14. The best ancient statues, such as Venus, Apollo, Laocoon, in order to familiarize themselves with the idea of classical beauty. 15. A good model and small figures for anatomy. 16. Prints, medals, paintings, engravings in black (obviously mezzotints) etc.

However, as the execution of the preceding plan demands a large space, the suppliant requests funds to build, sixty feet wide and as long as possible, in the new sections of the city. The suppliant has fixed his choice on the square closest to the first moat, near the place called the Tailor's Factory where there is a spacious rear entrance giving onto the street known as Ridderstaat where the suppliant will install a beautiful door bearing an appropriate

35 · Romeyn de Hooghe to the Burgermasters of Haarlem · 1971 · [69]

inscription and the names of their Lordships. The school being thus situated quite near the old part of the city, no one will be too far away. And if their Lordships were to accord the aforesaid plot to the suppliant, he would do the rest at his own expense and undertake immediately the organization of the establishment in order to show with the deepest respect that he is the

Messieurs the noble and
estimable Burgermasters'
Obedient & zealous servant,
Romeyn de Hooghe

The 5th of March 1688

·E·A·POE·
ANASTATIC
PRINTING

36 · Anastatic Printing · 1972 · [70]

THE DRAWINGS OF JACOB DE GHEYN II

BY J. RICHARD JUDSON

THE GEHENNA PRESS

NORTHAMPTON

MCMLXXII

Othello   Hath he said anything?
   Iago He hath, my lord, but be you well assur'd,
        No more than he'll unswear.
Othello   What hath he said?
   Iago Faith, that he did...I know not what he did.
Othello But what?
   Iago Lie.
Othello   With her?
   Iago   With her, on her, what you will.
Othello Lie with her, lie on her?-We say lie on her, when they
        belie her,-lie with her, zounds, that's fulsome!
        Handkerchief-confessions-handkerchief! To confess,
        and be hanged for his labour. First, to be hanged, and
        then to confess; I tremble at it. Nature would not invest
        herself in such shadowing passion without some
        instruction. It is not words that shake me thus.
        Pish! Noses, ears and lips. Is't possible?-Confess?-
        Handkerchief?-O devil! *He falls down.*

Iago Work on,

     My medicine, work: thus credulous fools are caught,

     And many worthy and chaste dames, even thus

     All guiltless, meet reproach. What ho, my lord,

     My lord, I say! Othello!...

                   Enter Cassio.

                        How now, Cassio?

Cassio What's the matter?

 Iago My lord is fall'n into an epilepsy,

     This is his second fit, he had one yesterday.

Cassio Rub him about the temples.

 Iago   No, forbear,

     The lethargy must have his quiet course,

     If not, he foams at mouth, and by and by

     Breaks out to savage madness: look, he stirs:

     Do you withdraw yourself a little while,

     He will recover straight; when he is gone,

     I would on great ocassion speak with you. *Exit Cassio.*

     How is it, general? have you not hurt your head?

Othello Dost thou mock me?

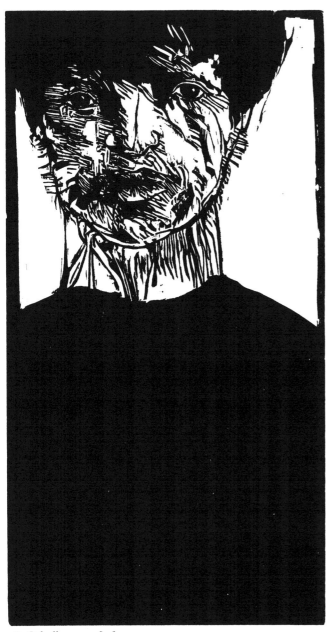

38 · Othello · 1973 · [75]

38 · Othello · 1973 · [75]

THE COAT WITHOUT A SEAM

SIXTY POEMS

1930 – 1972

STANLEY KUNITZ

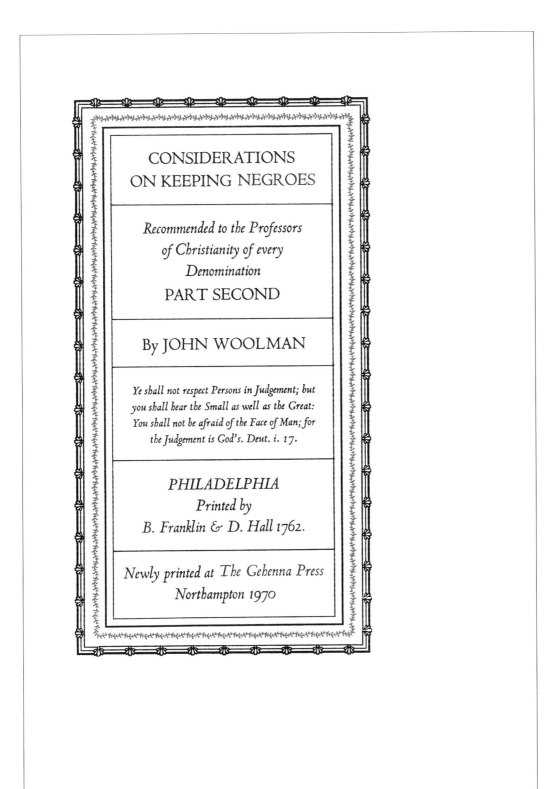

CONSIDERATIONS
ON KEEPING NEGROES

*Recommended to the Professors
of Christianity of every
Denomination*
PART SECOND

By JOHN WOOLMAN

*Ye shall not respect Persons in Judgement; but
you shall hear the Small as well as the Great:
You shall not be afraid of the Face of Man; for
the Judgement is God's. Deut. i. 17.*

PHILADELPHIA
Printed by
B. Franklin & D. Hall 1762.

Newly printed at The Gehenna Press
Northampton 1970

40 · Some Considerations on the Keeping of Negroes · 1975 · [78]

TED HUGHES
A
PRIMER
OF
BIRDS

WOODCUTS BY
LEONARD BASKIN

THE
GEHENNA
PRESS
1 9 · 8 1

41 · A Primer of Birds · 1981 · [80]

PHŒNIX

The funny Phœnix
Is no Sphynx
Rotting forever
In Egypt's stinks.

When his sun sets
He does not sulk
And sink in sands
His deathless bulk

But blazing in perfume
Like the morn
He eats himself roasted
And is reborn.

DIPTERA
A
BOOK OF FLIES
&
OTHER INSECTS

ETCHINGS BY LEONARD BASKIN
NOTE BY JOSE YGLESIAS
THE GEHENNA PRESS
MCMLXXXIII

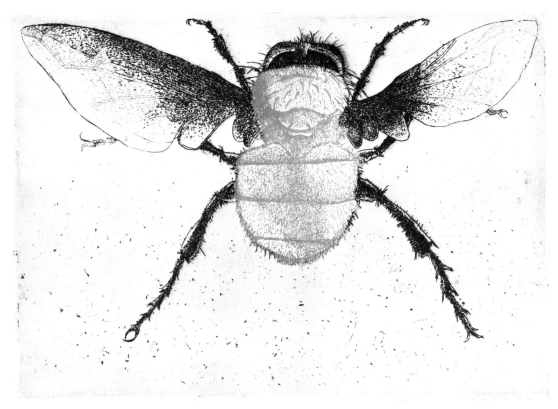

43 · Diptera · 1983 · [82]

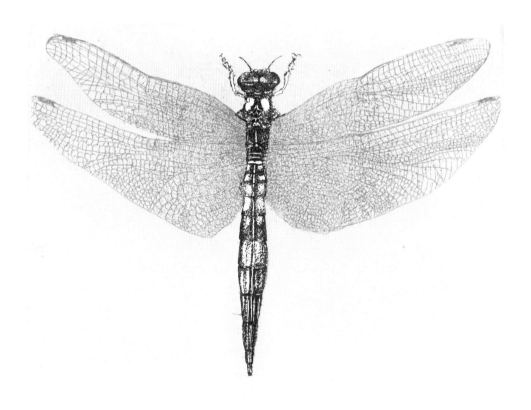

43 · Diptera · 1983 · [82]

VNKNoWN DVTCH ARTISTS

ETCHINGS AND BIOGRAPHICAL NOTICES
BY LEONARD BASKIN THE EREMITE PRESS

Romeyn Houtlucht was Seghers' only recorded
student, he spent four years in the painterly-
alchemical ambience of Seghers' studio, leaving
his master's attentions with arcane, now-lost
secrets in the primordial exercise of printing
with colour from metal plates. The dark corner
in which the likes of the mysterious Peter
Schenk or the obscure Johannes Ruisscher or
our Romeyn Houtlucht are historically tucked
away, is but rarely lit by Fortuna's revolving
searchlight and then made lambent only by the
luminescent presence of Hercules Seghers.
Crozats' account of his Haarlem visit to Teyler
of the celebrated Stichtung, describes inter-alia,
a sheaf of extraordinary etchings, printed in
colour, by Houtlucht. Crozat describes them as
transforming Seghers' coruscated, tone-
enchanted landscapes, into a profound
penetration of human morphology and
personality. Houtlucht is thus the arching
bridge-artist between Seghers and Rembrandt.

Adam Bloemaert, Abraham's elder
brother and uncle to Cornelis and Frederik
left Dordrecht at an early age, wandered about Europe
studying and mastering the verging neuroticisms of mannerism.
Whether he joined with Abraham in Utrecht is unknown; our knowledge
of Adam Bloemaert and his work is very scant, except for van Mander's
manuscript note in the copy of his "Het Schilder-Boeck" said to be in the
library of the Institute for Art History at Utrecht: that intriguing rubric
relates our painter's odd history. Scorning the commercialism of Utrecht's
burgeoning bourgeoisie he shed their traditions, conventions, customs, and
became a hermit. Van Mander found him in a wood near Arnheim, living
an entirely rude and haphazard existence at the mercy of natural
bounty and want. He had abandoned painting for study
and devotion but van Mander insists that he
kept his painting things by him.

MOKOMAKI

thirteen etchings

of shrunken & tatooed

Maori heads

by

Leonard Baskin

&

three poems

by

Ted Hughes

45 · Mokomaki · 1985 · [84]

45 · Mokomaki · 1985 · [84]

·ICONES·
·LIBRORVM·
·ARTIFICES·

·BEING ACTVAL· PVTATIVE·
FVGATIVE & FANTASTICAL
PORTRAITS OF ENGRAVERS·
ILLVSTRATORS & BINDERS·

·ETCHINGS AND NOTES BY
LEONARD BASKIN·

·THE GEHENNA PRESS·
·MCMLXXXVIII·

47·Icones Librorum Artifices ·1988 · [86]

Paris & Lyons were at mid-sixteenth century in close competition for palm-honours
in printing quality. Both had long-established traditions & in the celebrated hands
of Jean de Tournes & Simon de Colines a higher plane of sweet felicity & an enriched depth of grace were attained. Handsome typefaces & brilliantly fashioned printer's flowers & ornaments were displayed with apposite harmony & sustained sensibility. Typography, the art that preserves all
arts, is at its essence the arrangement & reordering of small elements, the manipulation of tiny nuances. Its vital measure exists only in subjective response to a gutter's width, to a he-
ading's depth, & in the aspect of the type as it spreads
across a page; the weight & feel of it. The crucial
minutiae are vested in niceties of judgement t-
hat decide the precise leading between lines, the type size, the number & place-
ment of the illustrations, the text
measure, & the disposition of all these elements in relation
to one another. How soul satisfying is a Suetonius by de Tournes or a Cicero by
Simon de Colines; they set paradigmatic standards that we put before us, to stimulate & instruct us.

· Jean de Tournes & Simon de Colines ·
· 16th c ·

·JOHANNES · TEYLER ·

·1648·1697·

By
daubing divers
colors into engraved
lines of a copperplate through the use of small rolled paper
stumps & then cleaning the polished surface with very great care, Johannes Teyler was
able to print many colors with a single pass through
the press. The French, who became very adept in this procedure,
called it printing à la poupée. Teyler, who was a Dutch engineer & professor of mathematics, used, for the most part, plates etched or engraved by
others, although his competence was acquitted and testified to by the etchings from
his identifiable hand. Hercules Seghers' wondrous prints, part painted and part printed,
were the only instance of printed color from metal plates before Teyler. Newton &
the knowledge of three color process belonged to Le Blon, the Gautier D'Ag-
otys and the later eighteenth century. Teyler's remarkable ability
and brilliance in deploying his primitive means can be seen
to great advantage at the British Museum in the mounted collection of proofs called 'Opus Typochrom-
aticum'. There were half-hearted efforts
to induce the secrets of printed col-
or from metal. The results
are not memorable and
all are virtually
unknown
now.

Surely, Maria Sibylla
Merian's books are all aglow; her
'European Insects' arrayed in brillant coloring, drive their haphazard flights through dazzling
florilegia, wanting only in scents. Her Surinamese metamorphosing insects are set in wondrous tropical color. Insects and the plants they symbiotically thrive with are rendered in the crushed-jewel-like color of their jungle habitat. The
intrepid Maria S. Merian braved the long and arduous 17th
century voyage to the dense heat-drenched world of Surinam
in Dutch Guinea. Combining meticulous, near-scienti-
fic observation & a vision profoundly touched by a
poetic perception of nature, she created an ex-
acting entomology, which although
conceived through lay-
ered veils of beauty,
pushed the knowledge and study
of insect life and habitat to new levels of
understanding. Here is a rare coupling of science & art, framing a beneficent dialectic in which the science is enhanced and the art is enlarged.
The folios which hold her painted engravings reta-
in the fresh, original colors, as they are firmly
shut away from the color-devouring light. Thus they glow with their original vivacity.
This merging of strength & delicacy is near unique.
· MARIA · SIBYLLA · MERIAN ·
· 1647 · 1717 ·

Anne Allen was mar-
ried to Jean Baptiste Pillement,
the unrivalled 'ornamentiste' of his age.
Her forty seven etchings are glowing color
reproductions of his floral and chinoiserie designs. The etchings are printed in radiant col-
ors. Nothing is known of Anne Allen's life; her work appears as
though sprung unheralded from Zeus; there is no proof that she was married
to Pillement. Everything but these forty seven ravishing etchings is steeped in a dark-
ened obscurity. Using the à la poupée technique with strenuous inventiveness & ingenuity,
tinged with uncommon delicacy & subtlety, the resulting prints are marvels of complex col-
or printing. Resorting to any device that would further heighten the quality of her prints, she
ingeniously used two copperplates to generate the greatest possible deployment of color. To add
further luster to her work, she took quick advantage of the new tendency to tint papers in the
subtlest shades of blue. With wondrous dexterity, Anne Allen's sensibilities enabled her
to manipulate this difficult, cumbersome, even crude printing method to astonishing
intricacy. The 'Cahirs' as she called these suites of prints often are composed of
sprays of flowers sprawling within a ragged Rococo context. They
shimmer and gleam with that special pellucid-
ity, a unique characteristic of color printed
from metal plates. Allen's glittering is indeed many hued and golden, unforgettable, and altogether unlike all other great color prints.
· ANNE · ALLEN ·
· fl. 1780 ·

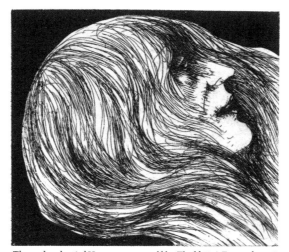

The wondrously gifted Housmans were an odd lot. The eldest, A.E. was a bitter &
secretly savage Oxonian Latinist whose famous poem was 'rue laden'; Laurence,
the middle sibling, abandoned a brilliant and well-established career as an illustrator, claiming his eyes could not stand the severe strain his close drawing style
put them to, and became famous as a writer; Clemence is the most elusive of the
three. This long-lived suffragist wrote the 'Werewolf', John Lane, 1896, &
she was a professional reproductive wood engraver, one of the last, it is said,
to be trained in England. She magnificently engraved Laurence's designs
for her own book & the drawings for most of his other books, which did
not exploit process blocks. Clemence's engravings are marvels of clarity and beauty. It may be said, and indeed Guthrie does aver,
that the special and entrancing qualities of The Pear Tree
Press illustrations are in large measure due to Clemence's sensitive and capable hand transfer-
ring Guthrie's designs into compelling works of fine art.
· CLEMENCE · HOUSMAN ·
· 1861 · 1955 ·

TWELVE SCVLPTORS

A BOOK OF MONOTYPES

WITH SHORT NOTES

ON THE MONOTYPES &

THE SCVLPTORS BY

LEONARD BASKIN

THE

EREMITE

PRESS

1988

RVSH

WARD

SAINT-GAVDENS

RIMMER

FRENCH

MACMONNIES

VONNOH

FLANAGAN

NADELMAN

LACHAISE

O'CONNOR

·L·B·

with etching, it infected the upper & royal classes with a mad enthusiasm for etching. Queen Victoria etched, as did many ladies-in-waiting & scores of others. This "epidemic of amateurism" & its works could not abide nor survive the hand-wiped classic copperplate printing procedures, no, it insisted upon veils of tone, floods of grey mist to befog the ineptitude, the awkwardness, the charming futility of the work. How odd that this need of the unlettered coincided with a strong trend amongst the professionals. The leading etching printers, especially at Paris, developed a mystique of tonal printing: it was said of Delâtre, its chief exponent, that he deployed "mysterious mud." The obsessive delight in retroussage, the rage for tonal atmosphere & surface mystery, for a deluge of obscurant shades, attained its zenith in the work of the Vicomte Lepic. He declared "I make prints as a painter not as a printmaker." Deltail reports that Lepic "obtained ninetyfive different impressions from the same plate of 'Vue des Bords de l'Escaut'." An indefatigable pursuer of tonalities, Lepic ultimately abandoned etching & painted directly onto the plate & rolled it & dampened paper through the etching press, & the monotype was reborn for the third time. Lepic & Degas were friends; Degas' first monotype also bears the name of Lepic who inducted him into the mystery. The monotype sharply suited two of Degas' gifts, superb draughtspersonship & his wonderful capacity for composition; indeed, Degas became the preeminent modern maker of monotypes. Beginning in 1860 he formed well over two hundred different monotypes. By painting, wiping, cleaning, & maneuvering the oil pigments on a plate, Degas could establish general suggestive forms which

Delâtre

Vicomte Lepic

Edgar Degas

had the potential to be altered or clarified later. Once he applied his gorgeous pastels to the monotype base, all the intended & accidental implications of the printed grease attained ultimate fulfilment. After Degas, the monotype became an available graphic device. Gaugin & Pissarro made quick & beautiful use of it as did many others. There would be, in this context, little purpose to my further rehearsing the known subsequent history of this wonderful means for modest replication. The medium was brilliantly employed in the post-academic furor of the fin-de-siécle; original, inventive & personal devices were devised & the medium's history down to our times is replete with resolutions & solutions that are pertinent to the maker's place & time. It would be usefully enlarging to digress here & discover the specifics of monotypic multiplication & other qualities inherent in the medium. It has always been the tendency of the monotypist to pull several other impressions after the first pass through the press. That first pass yielded a proof fully charged with ink or paint, a sufficiency of ink remained on the plate & the second or cognate impression was made, & then the third or ghost impression: thus classical procedure. Through the subtle manipulation of the pressure on the rollers of an etching press it is easily possible to double the number of classical impressions. When the plate is gravid, laden with pigment, the least possible pressure is used which gives-up a rich impression, then three cognates, each successive pull with a slight increase of pressure as concomitant to the loss of paint, the same again for the two ghosts, & finally with very intense pressure, virtually all oil, ink, grease is removed from the plate. Along with the mastery of differ-

Cognate
Ghost

49 · Irises · 1988 · [91]

49 · Irises · 1988 · [91]

50 · Fancies · Bizarreries & Ornamented Grotesques ·
1989 · [92]

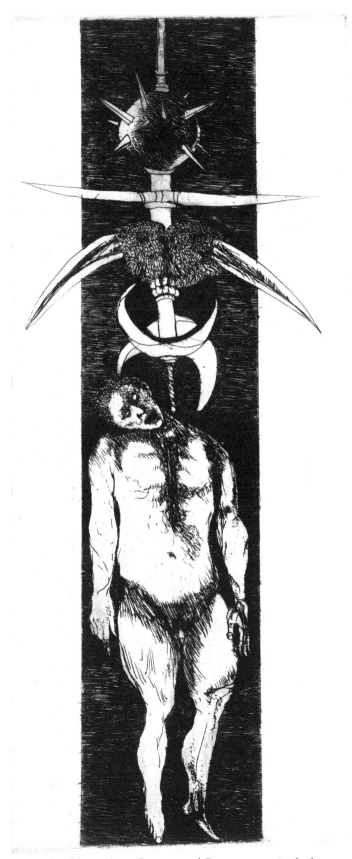

50 · Fancies · Bizarreries & Ornamented Grotesques · 1989 · [92]

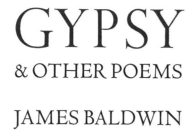

GYPSY
& OTHER POEMS

JAMES BALDWIN

THE GEHENNA PRESS
MCMLXXXIX

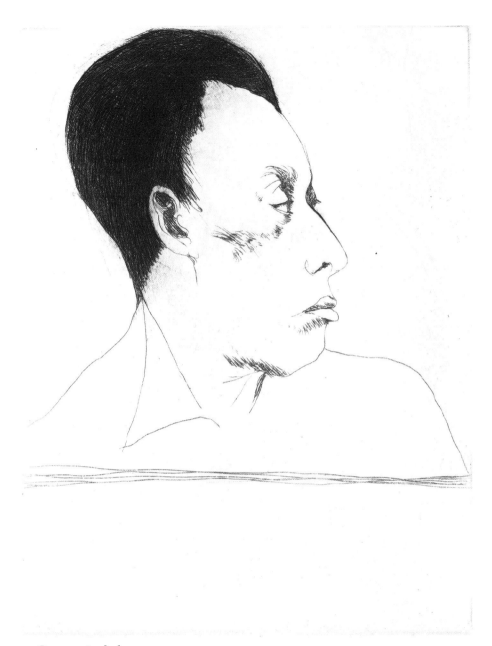

51 · Gypsy · 1989 · [93]

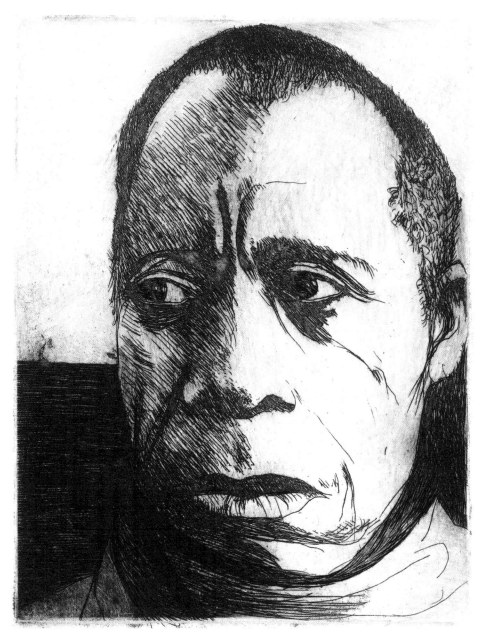

51 · Gypsy · 1989 · [93]

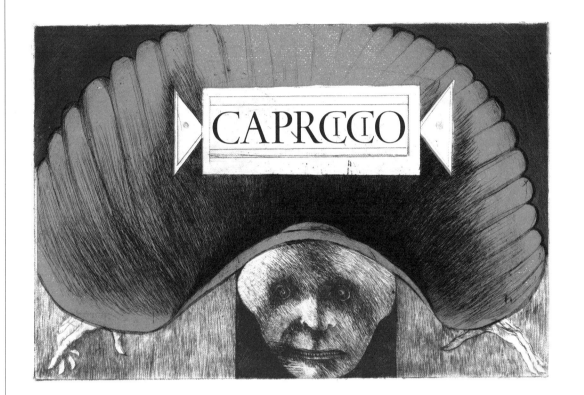

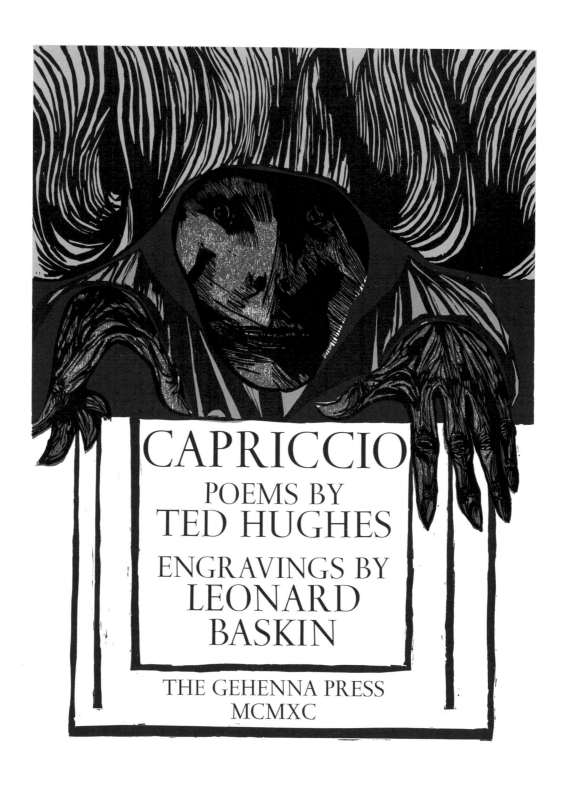

CAPRICCIO
POEMS BY
TED HUGHES

ENGRAVINGS BY
LEONARD
BASKIN

THE GEHENNA PRESS
MCMXC

52 · Capriccio · 1990 · [95]

52 · Capriccio · 1990 · [95]

52 · Capriccio · 1990 · [95]

52 · Capriccio · 1990 · [95]

52 · Capriccio · 1990 · [95]

SIBYLS

A BOOK OF POEMS
BY RUTH FAINLIGHT

WOODCUTS
BY LEONARD BASKIN

THE GEHENNA PRESS
MCMXCI

53 · Sibyls · 1991 · [96]

54 · Grotesques · 1991 · [97]

BASKIN

54 · Grotesques · 1991 · [97]

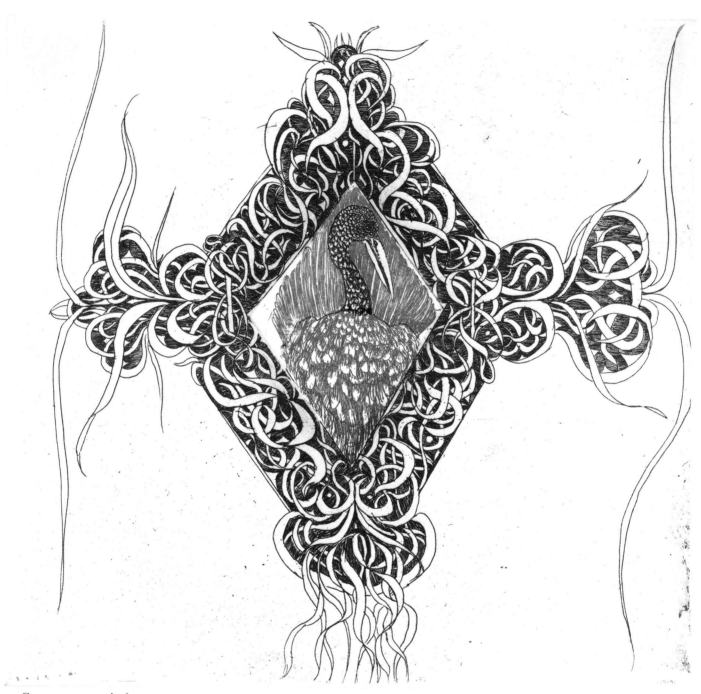

54 · Grotesques · 1991 · [97]

PRESSMARKS

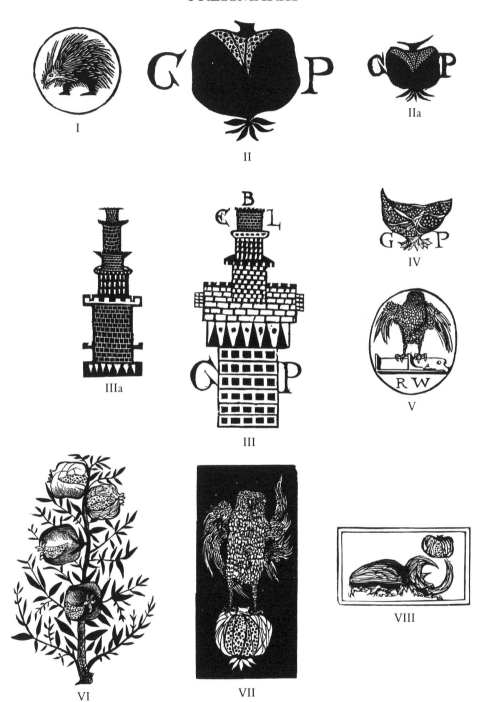

I

II

IIa

IIIa

III

IV

V

VI

VII

VIII

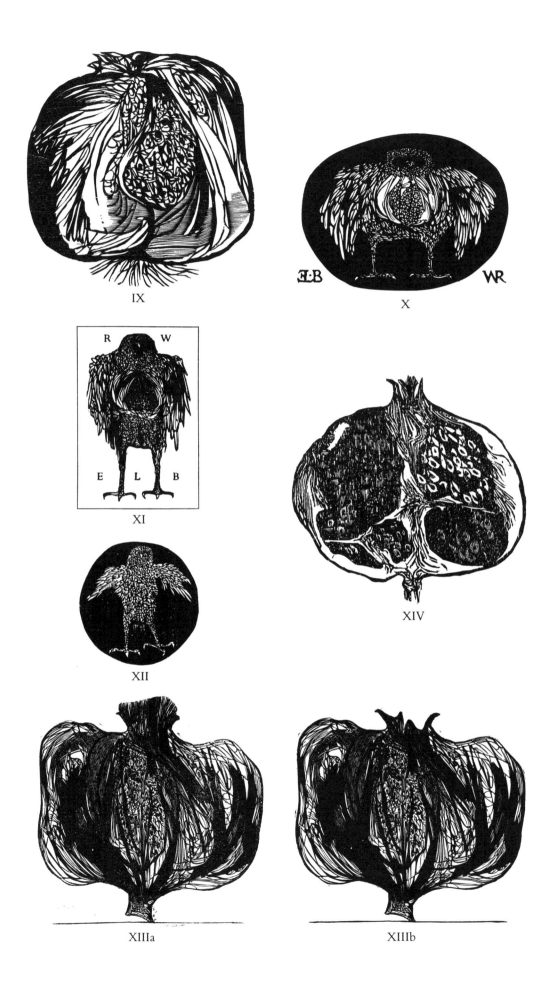

IX

X

XI

XII

XIV

XIIIa

XIIIb

XV

XVI

XVII

XVIII

XIX

XX

XXI

XXII

XXa

XXIII

XXIV

XXb

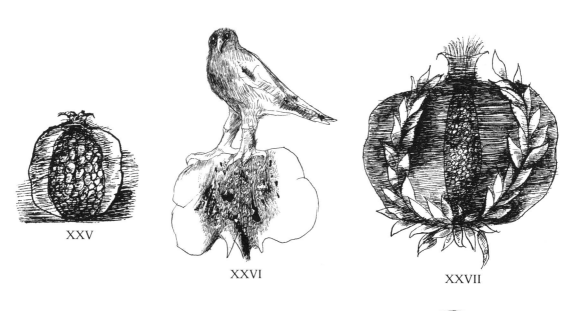

XXV

XXVI

XXVII

XXVIII

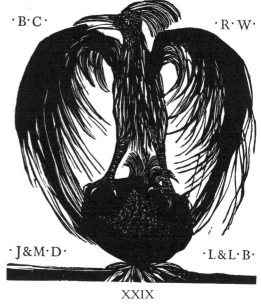

·B·C·   ·R·W·

·J&M·D·   ·L&L·B·

XXIX

XXX

XXXI

XXXII

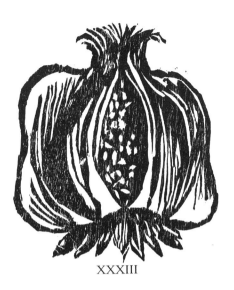

XXXIII

XXXIV

XXXV

XXXVI

XXXVII

XXXVIII

XXXIX

Two thousand copies of this catalogue have been printed by
the Oxbow Press, Amherst, Massachusetts. The typeface
used throughout is Bembo & was set by Linda Figovsky.
The design is by Leonard Baskin.
February, MCMXCII.